DATE DUE

the corporate promotables

the

corporate

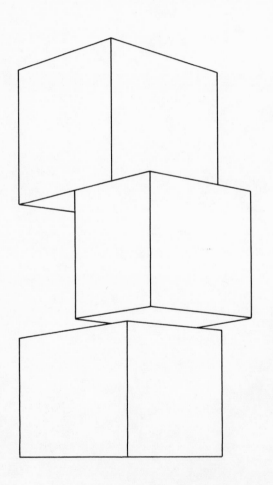

promotables

sexton adams

Associate Professor
School of Business Administration
North Texas State University
Denton, Texas

don fyffe

Division Commercial Supervisor
Southwestern Bell Telephone Co.
Lubbock, Texas

GULF PUBLISHING COMPANY
Houston, Texas

To Leta and Patsy

acknowledgements

We are indebted to many people for their contributions, suggestions, and support during the preparation of this book. Special thanks go to Vince Luchsinger, Chairman of the Department of Management, Carlton Whitehead and Louis Ponthieu, Professors of Management, and Louise Luchsinger, Professor of Marketing, all of Texas Tech University, who read portions of the manuscript and offered many helpful suggestions. We are also grateful to Fred Williams, Professor of Management, North Texas State University, for reading and commenting on several chapters.

Many managers and organizations cooperated with us fully in a highly sensitive research project. Their participation and assistance made this book possible.

We wish to thank the Humble Oil and Refining Company and the American Telephone and Telegraph Company for allowing us to publish descriptions of their management-assessment programs.

We are further indebted to Mr. Charles Vervalin and Mrs. Phyllis Harnsongkram of Gulf Publishing Company for their expert assistance in molding the manuscript into a readable book.

Finally, our most sincere thanks is reserved for our wives for sharing with us the agony and joy in writing this book.

Don Fyffe, Lubbock, Texas
Sexton Adams, Denton, Texas

table of contents

xi

appendix two

introduction

Who are the Corporate Promotables? Why are they promotable? Or not promotable? What qualities do the promotables possess—and the nonpromotables lack? How high in the corporate structure can they rise with what qualities?

Is promotability an accurate measurement of managerial ability? Is it based on such objective criteria as dedication, loyalty, technical knowledge, and hard work as most managers assume? Or is it only a statistical measurement of personal advancement?

What are the pitfalls to be avoided and the qualities to develop for promotability?

Many factors—conscious and subconscious—affect the selection of individuals for promotion. One comprehensive survey of several thousand business executives,[1] for example, examined the subject of promotability. The author emphasized that one factor complicating executive selection is the *unwritten law* which has evolved through the years concerning the essential qualifications for each step of the organizational hierarchy. These informal qualifications often develop into the real determinants of promotability within the organization and are often outside the company's formal appraisal programs.

The question "What kind of talent do we want in our company?" has often been answered with the selection of the *organization man.* This conformity has been attacked by many critics of management. They have indicted the organization man for his blind conformity, with few coming to his defense. Many writers have referred to him as a man caught in the pressures of conformity in large impersonal organizations. One group of writers, however, has shown insight into the realities of organizational life in its analysis of the organization man:

good

> ... Most organization men consciously want to be a cooperator, a human relator, and a team player because these are the means for accomplishment in our society as well as for personal success with less discomfort for all. Where he adjusts well, the organization man moves into a satisfying and exciting world where he can get things done.

> Faced with the choice of fighting the organization or working with it, the organization man's best chance at being himself—of giving free play to his intellect and vigor—lies in climbing aboard the steam-roller and trying to steer it, rather than standing quixotically in front of it and defying it. Yet this latter course, we might infer from the current literature, is exactly what he should do if he is to retain his integrity as a man.[2]

How promotability is related to conformity and individualism has been of major interest to the authors. Indeed, this interest has led to the development of this book. In our talks with executives, we found a great interest in, as one executive put it, "What it really takes to get ahead." Most companies are concerned not with blind conformity or love of individualism as such but with the question of determining an acceptable balance within the organization between company interest and individual interest.

The promotable executive needs to be an organization man since he has to have enough self-interest to adapt to organizational expectancies as well as to develop the necessary qualifications (either formal or informal) to move ahead in management ranks. Often managers are put in the uncomfortable position of having to choose between self-interest and company interest. This can be clearly seen in the dilemma of one young executive:

> I'm in charge of the computer operation here, and while we do some programming for specialized jobs, most of the programs are provided by our computer methods group at the home office. Well, they revised some procedures recently, and I got a letter down the pipe asking us to make a minor program patch to cover this for our local operations. They do this once in a while. And as I was checking the machine logic, I

saw something was wrong, so I checked out the whole program, and sure enough about a third of it was totally meaningless.

Now this causes quite a problem. It's costing us maybe a couple thousand a year here, let alone the other plants using the same program, and we've been using this program for about six years. What I've got to do is to figure out what to do about it. The first reaction, you know, is just prepare a routine recommendation pointing it out—but it's not that simple. I mean I've gotten myself in a bind, or could if I'm not careful.

You've got to figure what's going to happen when I point this out, since some headquarters people are going to want to know why we've been doing this all these years and nobody caught it before, and why the methods people didn't figure out how to simplify it from the start. And that's not all. The methods people will have to check out the whole program, which is a lot of extra work.

But with expenses the way they are, I really ought to get this straightened out. It's just that it's going to stir up a lot of trouble and some of the higher-ups are going to wish I'd kept my big mouth shut. I really don't know what to do—I wish I'd never found the damn thing. I guess I'll go ahead and do it but I don't like it. It's no way to get popular around here.

This points out the complexities of organization life. The question here is to what degree do companies demand the organization man or individualistic self-interest? At what point is the organization in trouble with too much conformity (or company loyalty) or too much self-interest on the part of its management? Obviously, the company is in jeopardy with either of these extremes.

The successful company requires a balance between these extremes to provide the environment in which company goals can be successfully reached. Integration of high degrees of self-interest with company goals calls for creative leadership on the part of management.

Theories of Leadership

The lack of creative leadership is a major problem in many organizations. Indeed, industry spends hundreds of thousands of dollars each year in programs to develop managers for leadership. Moreover, the search for and identification of potential leaders continues to engross the attention of chief executives across the nation.

Theories of leadership over the past 30 years have first emphasized certain traits of leadership, then concentrated on the particular situation requiring a form of leadership, and more recently have focused on leadership as a characteristic of groups or organizations.

The Trait Theory

Until the late 1940's, leadership research centered on certain traits of the individual as a leader. Aggressiveness, drive, loyalty, honesty, and initiative were thought to be characteristic of good leaders. Further, this "Great Man Theory" promulgated the belief that "leaders were born, not made." Later, the modified approach to the study of leadership acknowledged that traits could be learned through training and experience.

No wonder the trait theory gained wide acceptance. Leaders seemed to exhibit these traits, at least to some degree. But unfortunately, since these traits do exist in most people to varying degrees, no satisfactory explanation of leadership could be developed.

Several major weaknesses make the trait theory unacceptable. First, it did not include the influence of situational factors in leadership. Leadership cannot be understood apart from the environmental context—interaction with groups and individuals.[3] Second, social scientists have searched in vain for universal traits in leaders because it has not been possible to isolate specific traits common to all leaders.

Gouldner, in his study of leadership, points out additional weaknesses in this theory: (1) trait lists usually do not indicate which traits are most important and which are least important; (2) traits often are not virtually inclusive, such as in the case of judgement and common sense; (3) trait studies do not distinguish between traits which are needed for acquiring leadership and those which are necessary for maintaining it; (4) trait studies describe, but do not analyze, behavior patterns; and (5) the trait theory is based on debatable assumptions regarding personality.[4]

The Situational Approach

The situational approach replaced the trait theory and its unsuccessful search for universal leadership qualities. This new theory focused on the existence of leadership roles and skills which are evoked by situations in particular groups. Different situations involving different groups call for different styles or forms of leadership.

Where the trait theory centered on the individual, the situational approach centers on the interaction of people in groups. The group does have an important effect on the style of leadership effective during the problem situation. For example, the personal characteristics of the followers, the drives and needs of the group, as well as the characteristics of the manager and the organization—the structure and nature of the tasks to be done—all influence leadership.

A major weakness of the situational view of leadership is its failure to take into account that leadership is a very complex process in which the traits of individuals may very well play a part. Moreover, it does not sufficiently recognize the influence of the environmental context of the organization. Like the trait theory, the situational theories by themselves represent too limited and too extreme an explanation. Its advocates may be overlooking the possibility that at least some traits are required of potential managers if they are to advance within the organization.[5] In some firms, common traits of individuals at certain levels seem to be required for promotion. Actually, a theory of leadership can and probably does involve both traits and situations.[6]

In later chapters the environment in which potential managers work will be examined in greater detail because it does play an important part in the career of the promotable managers. But we can suggest what we mean by saying that the organizational climate most conducive to potential managers is objective in its philosophy toward its employees, in its appraisal of its executives, and in its promotion policies.

The Organization and the Individual

Companies often attempt to develop within their managers a high degree of creative leadership through executive development programs which may or may not be entirely successful.

Developing the Manager

There seems to be at least two schools of thought concerning the development of managers. The first concerns itself with management development—that is, management development programs, in-plant training, job rotation, multiple management and so forth. Many proponents of these programs argue that they develop proper attitudes and skills and that these programs will instill in the participants the necessary qualifications that the company deems important for success.

Much time and effort has been devoted to studies of successful executives in an attempt to determine those qualities required for success, and to in-depth analyses of case studies of companies. Other investigators have undertaken to define those managerial styles and approaches to management practices and people which are the most successful.[7]

Changing the Organization

The second school of thought concerning this controversy[8] suggests that it is much better to change the organization in order to create a challenging and permissive environment in which people can develop themselves. This argument contends that one serious fault of development programs is that they may accomplish little if the changed individual goes back into an unchanged organization in which he is unable to use his new-found skill.

Many argue for changing the rigidity of organizational philosophy. Douglas McGregor strongly supports this idea in *The Human Side of Enterprise*. His concept of integration—that is, tying individual goals to company objectives—is defined as, "The creation of conditions such that the members of the organization can achieve their own goals best by directing their efforts toward the success of the enterprise."[9]

Comparatively speaking, however, a more limited amount of effort has been spent in considering the appropriateness of the corporate environment. And nowhere in the literature is there a comprehensive evaluation of corporate objectivity as related to the individual manager and evaluation of the objectivity of the manager as related to his organization.

It is to fill this void that this book has been written.

Plan of the Book

The purpose of this study is to investigate how managers—the Corporate Promotables—achieve success within their organizations. Although there has been a wealth of literature on the subject of promotability, most of this research misses the mark in that it concentrates on the so-called traits that executives must have in order to be successful.

These studies omit the obvious. That is, they concentrate on separating the individual from his organization and on attempting to identify personality characteristics that may have been thought important in the past.[10] Moreover, some companies have attempted to develop a psychological profile by which to measure a manager's potential.

The major weakness of such approaches is that they minimize or overlook the terrific pressure that the organization exerts on the individual once he enters organizational life. The true measure of potential takes place within the organization when the individual adjusts to the role expectancies of the organization. Only within the organization, under fire, can the true mettle of executives be measured. For this reason, it is much easier to measure the results of an experienced manager than to measure the potential of inexperienced, unproven individuals.

With these points in mind, the authors studied three organizations, although many other companies were researched and material from those companies is integrated in our analysis. We attempted to study the successful executive within organizations and to determine why he was successful while others were unsuccessful, how the successful manager adapts to the organization's expectancies, and to observe the pressures applied to all managers by organizational life.

The first company studied, Wildcat Petroleum, Inc.,* is an independent oil company which may be characterized as a nongrowth organization. Originally founded on the opportunism of the early days of the oil industry, it has been steadily declining in sales and growth over the past few years. A study of the managers of this company provides excellent insights into the manipulation occurring within that company.

Our second company is Amalgamated Electronics, Inc., a large bureaucratic company with upwards of 70,000 personnel scattered within all geographic areas of the United States. Our study took place in a plant employing approximately 4,000 employees. Because of the company's bureaucracy and complex organization, the managers of Amalgamated provide an interesting study on organizational survival.

The materials for our third study were drawn from Diversified Manufacturing, Inc., a large widely known company with a well-recognized dictatorial philosophy. Our Corporate Promotables within this organization are a different breed of executive than that found within Wildcat and Amalgamated. And yet, these managers act in a predicted manner to conform to the organizational expectancies and for their own success within the organization.

Our research into these three companies, as well as other companies, has disclosed a wide variance in corporate

---

*Fictitious names are used for the three major companies analyzed.

objectivity—the degree the company is interested in its own welfare. The degree of corporate objectivity is a principal consideration since it is this objectivity which determines the corporate environment to which the individual adjusts.

In addition, our probing revealed that the philosophies of the individual managers can be reduced to the basic form of a balance between self-interest and company interest. The organization has certain role expectancies for its managers. This expectancy may be thought of as the individual's self-company interest balance as related to his organization's anticipated actions and philosophies.

Means of measuring corporate objectivity, the manager's balance between self-interest and company interest, and the organization's expectancy are provided in Chapter 1. Considering the individual manager's adaptation to organizational expectancies and his self-company interest balance, we have expressed the potential promotability of managers as a mathematical formula. This promotability formula is explained and discussed within Chapter 1.

Chapter 2 focuses on a method of determining the individual manager's classification of managerial personality and style. The classifications include the Technician, the Dictator, the Executive, the Opportunist, and the Noncontroversial Conformist. Each classification is discussed in relation to the companies researched, and a clear picture of managerial philosophies, modes of operation, and abilities are presented within this chapter.

The promotables and their battlegrounds is the subject for Chapter 3. Background on the companies is presented along with organizational charts identifying managers and their classifications. The comments of executives provide the stage for understanding the corporate operational philosophy of each company. Subsequent chapters build upon the foundation presented here.

Management theorists for years have concentrated on the subculture of the organization as a focus for understanding the role of small groups within the company. Chapter 4 begins with a general explanation of the corporate culture as a subculture within American society. The subculture and its effects on the individual is discussed and analyzed for each company.

Based upon the background of the corporate subculture, Chapter 5 probes organizational informality. Official and unofficial actions as indicators of objectivity and nonobjectivity within the corporate structure are presented to show the complexity and intertwining of such actions within the typical organization. Horizontal, vertical, and opportunistic cliques are traced and related within each company.

Socionepotism is a necessary part of corporate cliques and may be significant in shaping the future of organizations. Another form of nepotism normally found within the organization, adoptive nepotism, occurs when some top-level executive *sponsors* another individual at a lower level. Any study of such action provides a very interesting insight into corporate life.

Chapter 6 deals with the power struggles that occur within these organizations and the effects of corporate bureaucracy on the organization. The schism between line and staff operations has long been a subject of management literature. The different philosophies and modes of operations of line and staff departments are again presented to show why power struggles occur.

The problems involved in the complex climb through the hierarchy are illustrated in Chapter 7. The differences between promotables and nonpromotables can be seen through the *busted-britches* effect and *dead-end* jobs which are discussed throughout this chapter. The effects of a lack of objectivity within the organization and within the individual are analyzed to illustrate why some managers fail.

The problems, attitudes, and philosophies of Corporate Promotables are classified and presented in a cluster from Chapter 8 through Chapter 12. Each chapter begins with an interview with a certain classification of executive who explains his personal operating philosophy; then the effects of his approach are shown. Chapter 8, for instance, presents a clear picture of the Dictator, his philosophies, and the effects of his approach on his organization.

Remaining chapters are concerned with the Noncontroversial Conformist, the Technician, the Opportunist, and finally the Executive. These chapters, like Chapter 8, emphasize the problems of managers as they operate within their companies.

Organizations often suffer because of their failure to either educate types such as the Technicians as to what is really expected of them or to correct the approach of the Dictator and the Opportunist who may be doing irreparable harm to the company. Organizations often seemingly close their eyes to the maneuvering of certain executives such as Opportunists or Dictators or Noncontroversial Conformists without weighing the cost to the organization.

Perhaps these organizations are not objective enough in evaluating and rewarding sound contributions, such as those made by the true executive. Chapter 12 presents the operating philosophy and the leadership style of the Executive.

Chapter 13 is a capstone and capsule summary of the Corporate Promotables. It explains why some managers are promotable and others are not. Data gathered from our investigations support the theory presented in the earlier chapters of the book.

Finally, Chapter 14 presents the challenge of the future. This concluding chapter discusses the mechanistic, humanistic, and modernistic organization theories and their effects on the philosophy of today's managers, and the need for perceptive and innovative management.

Literature Cited

1. Garda W. Bowman, "What Helps or Harms Promotability?" *Harvard Business Review,* XLII (January-February, 1964), 6.

2. Roger M. Bellows, T.Q. Gibson, and George S. Odiorne, *Executive Skills, Their Dynamics and Development* (Englewood Cliffs, New Jersey: Prentice-Hall, Inc., 1962), p. 263.

3. Thomas Gordon, *Group-Centered Leadership* (Boston: Houghton Mifflin Company, 1955), pp. 46-51.

4. Alvin W. Gouldner, ed., *Studies in Leadership* (New York: Harper and Brothers, 1950), pp. 23-24, 31-35.

5. Gordon, p. 49.

6. Gouldner, p. 35.

7. See, for example, Robert R. Blake and Jane S. Mouton, *The Managerial Grid* (Houston: Gulf Publishing Company, 1964).

8. For an interesting discussion of this issue see G. Strauss and Leonard R. Sayles, *Personnel, The Human Problems of Management,* 2nd ed. (Englewood Cliffs, New Jersey: Prentice-Hall, Inc., 1967), Chapter 22.

9. New York: McGraw-Hill Book Company, 1960, p. 49.

10. See William R. Dill, Thomas L. Hilton, and Walter R. Reitman, *The New Managers* (Englewood Cliffs, New Jersey: Prentice-Hall, Inc., 1962), pp. 3-7.

the corporate promotables

1 : corporate objectives and (vs.) individual self-interests

After the promotable manager moves from the lower levels of the organization, he meets aggressive competition for promotion. Success in meeting this competition determines his future promotability.

The upward-mobile manager[1] has pressures from above and below and from his peers. He is often unsure of how his work is being viewed—whether his work is good, bad or mediocre. Most of this uncertainty stems from unclear, unwritten, and varying criteria of job performance. He often has little direct satisfaction for a job well done since he may never see the clear-cut completion of a task.

Promotions serve as signs of success. The executive depends on the perceptions and interpretations of others, usually his superiors, for his job satisfaction. If he does not fit the organizational image of a higher-level executive, he may not move forward.

Informal Expectations

In attempting to adjust to his organization, an individual must determine both the formal and informal expectations. Often the informal qualifications or *unwritten laws* have developed over the years, forming an image of a promotable executive which may not agree with formal promotion policies.[2] Indeed, executives may discover that the stated expectations are in opposition to those actually desired.[3]

1

The following comments were made by a young college graduate who found himself in this situation:

> When they interviewed me prior to graduation, all the literature they handed out emphasized the importance of initiative, aggressiveness, and the ability to come up with new ideas. I guess maybe I'm just naive or something because I believed the recruiters really meant it. Until I went to work, that is. I had sense enough to keep my mouth shut at first, but as I learned, I could see several ways to improve production, and I talked to my boss about them. He just wasn't interested, and after several weeks he suggested I forget it and do my job like they've been doing it for years. I let it go for a while and then brought it up again. He got a little abrupt with me, saying for crying out loud, he'd known how to improve things for years, but we'd both be better off if I did what I was told and left the thinking to somebody higher up.

There are reasons for the variations in stated and desired expectations. The company interviewer is competing for capable graduates. He would hardly place his company in a competitive position if he explained in detail the actual operating philosophies of industry.

The following statement by a second-level manager in a large manufacturing concern reveals other reasons for the variations:

> I see these kids come and go, most make it but some don't, and I try to help them all I can. They don't understand what's expected of them, regardless if they are on our training program or come up from the ranks. They see something wrong, or at least think it is, and right away want to change it. It doesn't work that way, it's not that simple. In the first place, there may be good reasons we do something the way we do, and if not, chances are we have valid reasons for not changing it—maybe even something we don't want to talk about.
>
> I try to teach them that their job is to do the job assigned and to learn. Their chance will come to change things, but not until they've progressed a couple of levels. They have the men to contend with too. Some of these guys have been on the job for years and don't take kindly to some inexperienced kid telling them everything's wrong. Rub the men the wrong way and production is going to drop off. I tell them,

sure, be eager. Eager to learn and to work. But be humble. No smart aleck is going to make it. I preach to them all the time. Sometimes it helps, sometimes not. All I can do is try.

The older and more experienced executives attempt to inculcate the younger supervisors and managers with the proper attitudes required by their positions within the hierarchy. How well they learn determines their success at the lower levels of supervision. This learning process is one of the more serious personnel problems in industry since it is at the trial stage that many potentially capable individuals are separated from the organization, with loss to the individual and to the company.

Many company expectations are not so easily diagnosed, however. Dalton[4] reports in his study of "Milo," an industrial firm, that those wanting to advance had a better chance if they met the never-stated expectations of belonging to the proper fraternal organization and the proper yacht club and were Anglo-Saxon, Protestant, and Republican. And more importantly, these aspiring executives had to handle the rough and tumble of the in-fighting which went on throughout the organization.

Somewhat similar expectations were discovered in the companies we studied. Some emphasized interpersonal relationships, others conformity of dress,* the *proper* educational backgrounds, technical competence, or the intangible qualification of "getting along with people."

All firms had one thing in common—their desire for conformity to their standards, stated and unstated, formal and informal. This is in essence an attempt to adapt the organism (the individual) to his environment (the organization). Little, if any, thought has been given to the desirability of the environment.

Although much has been written about the necessity of creating an environment or company philosophy which allows

---

*An amusing example was discovered in our research of a major oil company. It seems that the *comers* in management always wore garters for their socks. The aspiring managers were told that if they hoped to "make it" in this company, they too would wear garters. (Whyte in *The Organization Man* cites many such examples.)

managerial self-development, little progress has been made in establishing how this may be done in large, bureaucratic enterprises. Hundreds or even thousands of organizations regard it as an impossible task to change such an intangible, subjective "thing" as the philosophy toward employees and managers. We disagree.

The Corporate Objectivity Quotient (OQ)

The following form was developed with the belief that if the company philosophy as perceived by its managers could be measured, then improvement could follow.

We suggest that the reader select the statement which describes his company's philosophy and measure it against the criteria developed in this chapter.

Company

Select one of the following descriptions most nearly representing what you think your company actually wants you to do. Do not consider what you think it should want or what you actually do.

1. Higher management likes for me to consider the interests of the company. They prefer that I don't suggest changes in procedures too often, however, since changes cause extra work and it just rocks the boat. The smartest thing for me to do in my company is take care of myself and let the company take care of itself.

2. Higher management wants me to always consider the interests of the company. They like for me to suggest changes in procedures when I see the need for it, if the changes are compatible with company policy and won't offend anyone higher up. I figure what's good for the company may be good for me, too.

3. Higher management expects me to help further the interests of the company. They like for me to suggest changes in procedures when I see the need for it, provided such changes

are not in opposition to company policy. In my company, I figure what's good for the company is usually good for me.

4. Higher management expects me to do everything I can to further the interests of the company. They want me to suggest changes in procedures when I see the need for it, and they appreciate my initiative. In my company, I figure what's good for the company is also good for me.

Organizations develop a personality. The formal organization blends with the informal to develop its own culture, traditions, and modes of action. Many companies are affected by the personal philosophy of top management and, as a result, may be efficient or sluggish, cold or warm, autocratic or democratic. An organization may attract people who fit its personality or may mold them to its philosophy.[5] The corporate personality can be recognized easily by the managerial staff as they either accept or reject it. The managers who do accept it are acutely aware of the philosophy and the company's expectations of them.

The preceding form provides a scale for measuring the philosophy of a company, or the degree of interest the company has in its own welfare, as viewed by the individual managers.[6] We will refer to it as the Corporate Objectivity Quotient (OQ).

The measurement of OQ as provided by the questionnaire gives four levels of objectivity (or the company's self-interest) from 25 percent through 100 percent. This assumes response 1 at 25 percent rather than 0 percent, since it seems doubtful that an organization could exist with a total lack of self-interest. Response 4 at 100 percent is, of course, an approximation since no firm is 100 percent objective.

The most accurate method of determining the OQ is to average the answers of a representative sampling of middle managers or, preferably, the complete middle-management team. The lower-level managers often, through inexperience, cannot accurately judge the company. Upper managers are sometimes, though certainly not always, reluctant to criticize their companies since they may view this as self-criticism. The researchers relied on this method, using the middle management team for determination of corporate objectivity, since it proved more reliable than other methods.

There is a wide variance in the Objectivity Quotient of organizations. Most young and expanding firms have a high OQ; however, firms, like people, tend to reach their maximum growth, stabilize, and gradually grow old. The OQ diminishes throughout this *natural* evolutionary process.

Large bureaucratic organizations which have existed for some time also vary in objectivity and almost without exception have a lower OQ than young and growing firms. Some of these firms, however, are still experiencing rapid expansion and their OQ is higher than that of other comparable firms.

Without exception, the established firms with relatively high OQ's had methods—or corporate philosophies—designed to maintain the OQ at levels acceptable to the firms. These were often stated as formal policy with related methods of enforcement, such as effective internal auditing for honesty.

Of more significance, however, is the policy requiring interest in the organization as a prerequisite to promotability.[7] In this case, then, self-interest is equated with company interest. The resulting conditions are complex and involve the formal and informal company directives and philosophies and the interpersonal relationships both formal and informal—the corporate subculture.

Actual Balance (AB)

Self-interest is a strong motivator. In fact, for many executives it may be the paramount one. In commenting on the Principle of Self-Interest, Jay observes:

> You may think that if you take a man on, give him a guarantee of employment, a fair salary, and a well-defined job, you can assume from then onward that he will work for the good of the corporation which is employing him. Perhaps there are some who do. But on the whole it is safer to assume that while the good of the corporation will always be an

important consideration, it will not be his first loyalty: that is reserved for himself, for his present status and rewards and his future career.[8]

The hard-working, hard-driving executive with the company's interests always in mind has traditionally been regarded as being the ideal image of the promotable manager. In reality, the individual who continuously makes this effort for the good of the company may actually be reducing his long-run value to the organization by failing to gain adequate personal development.[9] The astute individual attempts to judge just how much ambitious self-interest and company loyalty is necessary for advancement.

The ambitious executive may need to moderate his drive. If he is openly self-centered, his fellow executives may refuse to cooperate because his ambition is regarded as a threat to their own security or advancement. Small wonder that the pressures for success may foster political ruthlessness and self-centered opportunism in the corporate promotable.[10]

He may use his self-interest in more subtle ways. For example, through the cultivation of friendships and working relationships, the use of the informal organization, and by developing his skills in corporate politics. But regardless of the method, the promotable executive mentally adjusts to the realization of what the organization expects of him. Thus, the executive's awareness and sensitivity to the environment plays an important part in his success.

The progress up the promotability ladder, according to Dill, Hilton, and Reitman, " . . . depends greatly on the strategy or heuristics that an individual employs in 'his game' with the organization environment that he encounters at work."[11] They argue that the executive who wants to get ahead must behave with the necessary social and political attitudes and actions in light of his perception of the tone of the organization. He must look to himself in promoting his career and be constantly aware of both the subtle human nuances around him and his timing in applying the appropriate tactics in his campaign for promotion.

Self-interest may be viewed as a combination of the psychological drives of achievement, ego, and power, the true motivators of most top executives.[12] We will use the term *self-interest* when referring to these psychological drives.

In its most basic form, the occupational philosophy of the individual can be expressed as the balance between self-interest and company interest—the Actual Balance (AB).

The Actual Balance is determined from the following scale. Again, the reader may measure his Actual Balance by selecting the most descriptive statement of his philosophy.

Self

Select one of the following descriptions which most nearly represents what you actually do. Do not consider what you think your company wants you to do or what you think you should do.

1. I act in the best interests of the company even if it may not be the smart thing for me personally. I can't stand to see things done the wrong way. I do all I can to correct them, even if the corrections won't contribute to improved results on my own job. I think I owe the company my loyalty and best efforts.

2. I usually act in the best interests of the company even if it may not always be the smart thing for me personally. I don't like to see things done the wrong way. I usually do something to correct them, even if the corrections don't help me on my job. I think I owe the company quite a bit of consideration.

3. I act in the best interests of the company as long as it is usually in my interests, too. I don't like to see things done the wrong way. I sometimes do what I can to correct them, especially if the corrections contribute to improved results on my own job. I try to strike a balance between taking care of the company and myself, since I can contribute more to the company in the long run if I consider myself too.

4. I often act in my own best interests which is usually in the best interests of the company too. I don't like to see things

done the wrong way. I sometimes do what I can to correct them, particularly if the corrections contribute to improved results on my own job, and provided they don't adversely affect me. I often think in terms of what is best for me, since I can contribute quite a bit more to the company in the long run if I consider myself too.

Although each manager's response to the above scale can be used in determining the Actual Balance, more accurate results are obtained when a knowledgeable ranking executive or personnel director who knows the managerial staff well determines each one's operating philosophy. Often, in large companies with large managerial staffs, several executives participated in this appraisal. The key executives' appraisals were then correlated with confidential group appraisals in which executives of similar organizational levels rated their fellow managers. Our research findings were obtained in this manner.

Response 1 indicates almost total interest in the company and little self-interest. Response 2 shows more company than self-interest. The choice of 3 indicates an almost even balance between self-interest and company interest. Response 4 indicates almost total self-interest.

Self-interest may be constructive or opportunistic, and may or may not be in the best interests of the company.[13]

Constructive Self-Interest

Constructive self-interest helps the individual adapt to his organization.

Some examples are formal or informal education, proper grooming, development of the necessary social skills, dedication and loyalty to his company as required for acceptance and promotability, and adapting to the reasonable expectations of his company. Anything the employee does to help himself which is also in the best interests of his company is constructive self-interest.

Opportunistic Self-Interest

Opportunistic self-interest is believed by the individual to be in his best interests, but is not in the best interests of his company. Some examples include attempting to use personal relationships for his advancement; obtaining results for the company which are expected but which he knows are not in the best interests of the company; falsifying reports or measurements; thinking and acting in terms of what he believes is best for himself without reference to the welfare of the organization; and of course, basic dishonesty.

Company Interest

Company interest is the individual's concern for the welfare of his organization. This is in the best interest of the company. It may or may not be in the best interest of the individual. When the individual's self-interest and company interest are synonymous, it is constructive self-interest.

Interest in the welfare of the company, however, may not be in the best interests of the individual. The following are examples of company interests that are not in the interest of the individual: suggesting changes in procedures which benefit the company but which will result in criticism to the individual for "rocking the boat"; and being dedicated and loyal to the company when the company rewards those who do little, are "nice guys," "apple polishers," or show opportunistic tendencies.

Not surprisingly, our research revealed that the difference between self-interest and company interest is related to the company's objectivity. In companies with high objectivity, self-interest is almost equated with company interest. Therefore, an individual's Actual Balance must be viewed in relation to his organization.

An excellent example of the close relationships which may exist between self-interest and company interest was obvious in one of the companies investigated. One young, progressive, chemical firm has experienced rapid growth in the past two years with financial gain to most of its top and middle executives who own stock in the company. When tested, these managers indicated a high degree of company loyalty. The reason is obvious. The company's gain is their gain.

One of the most revealing outcomes of the research is that the average self-interest increases from the lower to the higher levels of management through upper-middle management and then plateaus. Those who are most highly promotable in any organization, as proved by the higher levels they have attained, have on the average a higher degree of self-interest than do those at each succeeding lower level of management. This is true regardless of how low or how high the Objectivity Quotient of the organization.

Differences in individual self-company interest are revealed by the following statements. The first statement was made by an executive from an older, stable company that believes in taking care of its people.

> I'll tell you how to get ahead in this company. You have to get along with everybody, since you get promoted for what people think of you, not what you do. And you sure don't get a reputation for being a nice guy by stirring up trouble. In this business nice guys finish first.

A department manager in another company said:

> I do all I can to get our production up and keep it there, and I try to keep the men happy. The company doesn't like losing people, it costs too much to train new ones. It doesn't matter how you operate so long as it's fair, and the guys getting ahead are the ones who work at it, get good results, and really take an interest.

An upper manager's philosophy was expressed in this way in a third organization:

> I think that a man has to take care of himself, prepare himself if he wants to get ahead. And it's not always easy. If I get a chance at doing something that will get me noticed, so much the better, but I don't push it too hard. I try to get along with the other executives at this level, and I've found you can sometimes get more done over a cup of coffee or socializing at cocktail parties than you can by knocking heads

over a conference table. Nobody's going to take care of me but me, that's my responsibility, but I have responsibilities to the company too. If we didn't figure it that way, maybe there wouldn't be a company, and then where would we be?

The Expectancy Balance (EB)

The degree of self-interest required for promotability can be expressed as the company's Expectancy Balance.[14] It varies with the levels of the organization.

At the beginning of this chapter we quoted a young college graduate at the first level of supervision. He was expected to devote himself principally to the interests of his company.

In other companies, we found the same expectations, as seen in the following comments of a young foreman in an industrial firm: "To get promoted, I've got to keep my people happy and working. I'm expected to take the initiative in doing more than is necessary on the job." This is typical of the first two levels of all those companies tested which have five or more levels of supervision. In companies with four or less levels, the generalization applies to the first level only.

The self-interest required for promotability is generally a 2 on the Actual Balance scale at the first and second levels in large companies, and at the first level in small companies. The Expectancy Balance is therefore a 2 for these levels. This was true of the firms researched, although there may be some variation in other companies. Any knowledgeable executive should be able to recognize his company's expectations.

At the third and higher levels (second for companies with four or less levels of supervision), the self-interest required for promotability is either a 3 or a 4 on the Actual Balance scale. An exception to this is third-level *permanent* staff in large bureaucratic organizations who are usually 2's on the scale for reasons which will be discussed later.

Statistical data presenting the Actual Balance by classification, the degree of promotability by classifications, and promotability by Actual Balances are covered in Chapter 13.

The Promotability Quotient (PQ)

The degree of an individual's potential promotability can be expressed in the following formula.

PQ = 100 ± (EB - AB) x 50
PQ = the Promotability Quotient
EB = the Expectancy Balance expressed as a 2, or 3, or 4
AB = The Actual Balance expressed as a 1, or 2, or 3, or 4

The 100 is a constant. The difference between the EB and AB is multiplied by 50 in consideration of the four levels of self-interest and the three possible degrees of difference. This sum must be added to or subtracted from the constant of 100 to arrive at a score between 0 and 100.

For example, a person with an AB of 2 as measured by the AB scale in a company with an EB of 2 for his level would have a PQ of 100 as follows.

PQ = 100 ± (EB - AB) x 50
PQ = 100 ± (2-2) x 50
PQ = 100 ± (0)
PQ = 100

A PQ of 100 means that the individual has a high degree of potential promotability since he fits in well with the philosophy of his firm at his level of the organization. This requires a 2 at the two lower levels and a 3 or a 4 at the third or higher levels.

A person with an AB of 2 in a firm with an EB of 3 for his level would have a PQ of 50.

PQ = 100 ± (EB - AB) x 50
PQ = 100 ± (3-2) x 50
PQ = 100 ± (+1) x 50
PQ = 100 ± (+50)
PQ = 50

This individual has limited promotability since he is not adjusting to the expectations or to the prevailing image of the promotable executive for his level. In this case he lacks sufficient self-interest.

An AB of 3 with an EB of 2 would have the same effect with too much self-interest.

A person with an AB of 4 in a firm with an EB of 2 for his level would have a PQ of 0.

$$PQ = 100 \pm (EB - AB) \times 50$$
$$PQ = 100 \pm (2\text{-}4) \times 50$$
$$PQ = 100 \pm (\text{-}2) \times 50$$
$$PQ = 100 \pm (\text{-}100)$$
$$PQ = 0$$

This unfortunate individual is fostering the wrong image to move ahead in his company. He is obviously operating with a self-centered philosophy at a level of the organization which requires much more company interest for promotability. This spells almost certain occupational doom, since these people are usually separated from the company due to the image projected or due to the failure of obtaining the desired results from subordinates who resist supervision.

The PQ's as tested in the firms researched have the following general significance as related to known degrees of promotability, both past, planned, and anticipated:

PQ of 100 = High potential promotability
PQ of 50 = Limited promotability
PQ of 0 = Questionable or no promotability

We must recognize that promotability is complex and is influenced by a variety of factors in the organization, as well as by the qualifications of the individuals. However, the PQ as a measurement of potential promotability has been shown to be generally valid in the companies tested and consequently is of more than superficial significance.

The explanation for this is that the degree of self-interest expected by the company encourages those who desire promotability to develop the required qualities and to adapt to the requirements of the organization.

Those individuals whose Actual Balances differ appreciably from the Expectancy Balances of their companies either do not recognize the significance of the EB, or do not care to attempt self-development or to adapt to the requirements of their firms.

Literature Cited

1. See Robert Presthus, *The Organizational Society* (New York: Vintage Books, 1965), pp. 164-204, for an excellent description of the characteristics of such executives.

2. Garda W. Bowman, "What Helps or Harms Promotability?" *Harvard Business Review*, XLII (January-February, 1964), pp. 6 ff.

3. William R. Dill, Thomas L. Hilton, and Walter Reitman, *The New Managers* (Englewood Cliffs, New Jersey: Prentice-Hall, Inc., 1962), p. 11.

4. Melville Dalton, *Men Who Manage* (New York: John Wiley and Sons, Inc., 1959).

5. Keith Davis, *Human Relations in Business* (New York: McGraw-Hill Book Company, 1954), pp. 117-118.

6. Rensis Likert believes that the way the individual perceives his company and the roles he plays in it is important. He also believes that it is possible to measure climate indirectly by the perceptions of the individuals whose behavior is being studied. See R. Likert, *New Patterns of Management* (New York: McGraw-Hill Book Company, 1961).

7. Douglas McGregor, *The Professional Manager*, eds. Warren G. Bennis and Caroline McGregor (New York: McGraw-Hill Book Company, 1967), p. 77.

8. Antony Jay, *Management and Machiavelli* (New York: Holt, Rinehart and Winston, 1967), p. 213.

9. R. W. Powell, "How Men Get Ahead," *Nation's Business*, LII (March, 1964), 60.

10. S. B. Niles, Jr., "The Management Politician," *Harvard Business Review*, XXXIX (January-February, 1961), 99-104.

11. William R. Dill, Thomas L. Hilton, and Walter R. Reitman, "How Aspiring Managers Promote Their Own Careers," *California Management Review*, III (Summer, 1960), 10.

12. Victor H. Vroom, *Motivation in Management* (New York: American Foundation for Management Research, 1965), pp. 15-17.

13. See Saul W. Gellerman, *Motivation and Productivity* (American Management Association, 1963), pp. 199-203.

14. See Lyman W. Porter and Edward E. Lawler III, *Managerial Attitudes and Performance* (Homewood, Illinois: Richard D. Irwin, Inc., 1968), pp. 175-176.

2 : the promotables — who are they?

When the various managerial approaches and personalities of typical executives are classified, their effectiveness can be objectively evaluated. Our analysis has produced five basic classifications of promotable managers.

We suggest that the reader evaluate his managerial personality by selecting the statement which is most descriptive of himself.

Classification

1. I think I owe my company my loyalty and best efforts. I believe my primary responsibility is to do the best possible job I can in the best interests of my company. I devote myself to hard work to insure that my company's objectives are met.

2. I think I owe my company my loyalty and best efforts. I believe my primary responsibility is to lead my people in meeting our objectives, insisting that they meet them, and following up to see that we are successful. I devote my energies to obtaining or exceeding the results my company expects.

3. I think I owe my company my loyalty and best efforts. I believe my primary responsibility is in obtaining the best possible performance, and I've found that to do this you sometimes have to be just a little bit smarter and provide a little better leadership than others are capable of providing. I devote my energies to analyzing the opportunities in my

company for outstanding contributions and leading my people to superior performance.

4. I think I owe my company my loyalty and best efforts. I believe my primary responsibility is in providing an environment that is conducive to cooperative effort and that will permit my people to meet company objectives. I devote my energies to leading my people through harmonious efforts to insure that my company's objectives are met.

5. I think I owe my company my loyalty and best efforts. I believe my primary responsibility is in providing the leadership required to obtain the best possible performance through motivated people consistent with fair treatment. I devote my energies to constructive planning, development of managerial talent, and guidance of my people.

The Technician

Number 1 describes the Technician. He is company oriented and his approach is based on hard work, technical knowledge, experience and loyalty. He thinks in terms of what is good for the company and consequently may do little to prepare himself for promotability. He is often found in the staff organization.

The Technician is common in all companies, and we might question whether an organization could operate effectively without these *workers*. Their efforts are usually directed toward work, often hard work, and they seldom attempt to develop themselves for promotability after employment,[1] although college-graduate Technicians are common.

The term *Technician* is used as a personality type rather than as a definition of those people engaged in highly technical work such as chemistry or physics. Those so engaged may fall in any of the classifications.

Our analysis of the Technician is generally limited to those engaged in the line organizations or the operational staff organizations, that is, the staff people whose activities are directly related to support of the line functions. Peripheral staff organizations such as those concerned with research and development are not considered in detail.

The following comment illustrates the Technician's philosophy:

> I really dislike to see the way some people take advantage of the company, doing as little as they can. We're all in here to work or we're supposed to be. I don't mind doing my share, but I think everybody else ought to, too. At least I don't have to back up to get my paycheck. I earn mine.

In this example, the Technician justifies his occupational existence with hard work, but without emphasis on the quality of his contribution to the organization. Imagination and creativity are not mentioned and are probably not considered.

The following remarks made by another individual show another typical characteristic of many Technicians:

> The quickest way to foul things up is to try to change the rules as you go. If you deviate from the practices, you've set precedents, and that spells trouble. There's a reason we do things the way we do, based on experience and the combined knowledge of the people in this company, and I stick by the rules. It would work out better if everybody did.

The preceding example shows the conformity of the individual, although it possibly conflicts with his company's expectations. It also indicates the rigid thinking of many— although certainly not all—Technicians and the characteristic lack of imagination of many in this classification.

Some Technicians also lack aggressiveness and ambition:

> Staff life is a little slower and somewhat easier in this company. I know I'm not as ambitious as some people, but that's just the way I am. I don't like to push people when I'm not convinced it's necessary. I like to work at my own pace. I get more done that way than a lot of people do running around in mad circles. And I like to know my job, really know it in detail, better than anyone else. I'd go back to the line for a good promotion, but not for a lateral. I'd rather be out of the rat race.

The following comments indicate the emphasis placed on long hours as a method of proving loyalty and interest in the company.

> I work nights a lot trying to catch up. I don't like to get behind and I pound away until I get on top of the work. Many people clear out as soon as the shift is over. I figure a few minutes is not going to kill anybody.

The next quotation is typical of the Technician with high abilities who makes a contribution, sometimes an appreciable one, to his firm. He often attempts to earn promotions with this approach, which may not be effective in a firm with less than almost total objectivity—a situation he does not fully recognize.

> I have a good job here, one that is important to the company. Responsibilities accrue to those able to handle them, they say, and I keep getting broader assignments due to my willingness to accept responsibility and the technical knowledge I've gained over the years. The boss relies on me for a lot of things that properly should be handled by section heads who outrank me considerably, and this gives me some satisfaction. I'm respected for what I do here, and that means a lot to me.

The Technician tends to rely on hard work, experience, and loyalty, but probably his most significant trait is his general unwillingness to adapt himself to his organization's expectations or requirements for promotability. He does not attempt to adjust to the informal system of operations but usually prefers a straightforward and "by-the-book" approach.[2] He normally has limited ambition and is unwilling to make the sacrifices required for promotability.

For these reasons the Technician is seldom found above the second level of line organizations and third-level operational staff assignments.[3] Some Technicians reach the third level in staff organizations because of the need for stable, intelligent, and highly skilled staff managers.

The Technician adheres to the Protestant Ethic:[4] "By the sweat of our brows shall we earn our daily bread." Our American democracy was founded on this ethic, and it has been a part of our national heritage. Theoretically, hard work brings success. Our modern conspicuous consumption of the "fruits of our labors" encourages hard work for the enjoyment of material things.

Whyte suggests that the Protestant Ethic has given way in recent years to the Social Ethic. He argues that the present generation no longer believes that hard work is necessary for success, nor necessarily admires it. The emphasis has changed to the interpersonal relationships in an organization as the most important aspect of success.[5]

Although there has doubtlessly been a move away from the Protestant Ethic, the Technicians who make up a large percent of the management forces in industry continue to accept its premises. They will in all probability continue to do so in the future, not of conscious volition, but because the Technician finds it the path of least resistance. It is much easier for this type of person to work and be loyal than it is for him to adjust to an occupational philosophy that is incompatible with his philosophy and limitations.

The Dictator

Number 2 is the Dictator classification. The Dictator steps on toes, is aggressive, drives his people, is interested only in production, may be inventive, shows initiative, and his image is of one who fights to win and, perhaps rightly or wrongly, wins. He stands on his results and may be credited with results not actually attained. People seldom want to work for him. However, he is often a successful manager.

The Dictator is interested in results and his personal philosophy is directed almost entirely to obtaining the results expected or those he thinks are expected from higher management. He is ambitious and competitive and uses the results he obtains as a method of advancing in the organization.

As the top executive, the results he seeks are usually in the best interests of his company. If he is capable, he may be very successful as the head of his organization. Will Rogers once said that a dictatorship is the best form of government, provided you have the right dictator. This may very well apply to a business enterprise too, over the short run, but assurance that you have the right dictator is another matter.

Robert Sheenan in his analysis of Montgomery Ward[6] discusses Sewell Avery's administration which began in 1931. Avery is credited with saving the company during the depression of the thirties, but this experience had such a profound effect on Avery, and he had so little faith in the American economy, that he prevented the expansion of his company.

Ward's competitors, such as Sears, grew rapidly and consequently had a much larger share of the market. This continued until Avery's forced retirement in 1955 following the Wolfson proxy fight in which Wolfson was defeated.

Sheenan gave another example of a Dictator as the top executive. Safeway[7] enjoyed its prominent position in the retail-food industry largely as a result of the abilities of its top executive, Lingren A. Warren. But Warren's obsessive insistence on meeting all competitors' prices ultimately led to antitrust action by the Department of Justice in the Texas courts.

Warren also opposed the use of trading stamps and the demands of national-brand suppliers. In addition, he had his own ideas on store location and financing. He left the organization after some twenty years as the top executive.

The Dictator, like any other top executive, must hold lesser positions on his way to the top. His interest in results may or may not be in the best interest of the company, depending on whether the results required or assumed to be required are actually in the best interests of the company and whether the methods used to obtain them are compatible with company interest.

The following comments illustrate this point:

> I saw this one coming and I knew there would be hell to pay before it was over. It didn't take a genius to figure what would happen; the other section heads recognized it too. Collins wasn't familiar with our operations, hadn't been here long enough, and, of course, he had pressure on him [from the general office] to get production up since we didn't compare favorably with the other plants.

But it's not that simple, we're in a bind in our labor market, and we didn't have the experience in the line most of the other plants had. Under these circumstances, you can't get production up overnight. But when Collins asked, not insisted, just asked us to try to get it up, Johnson jumped in with both feet, said get production up. But the price we paid was high. We slacked off on maintenance and cut other corners. It worked for a while, but it soon caught up with us.

Johnson came unglued and started sending down directives—do this, do that—and tried to run it himself. The next thing you know he's got us spending all our time answering why we're in trouble, and we can't get out on the line to do anything. We start losing people, the experience factor gets lower and lower, so we need more people, but Johnson won't let us hire. By then we're in real trouble. The other department heads knew better than to crash it. They took it easy and came out O.K. Not us, we're just now coming out of it, and that happened almost a year ago.

The Dictator is sometimes prone to get results he knows are not in the best interests of his company, and in extreme cases he may be somewhat unconcerned about the methods. These results are, however, believed to be in his own best interests. He develops a reputation for action, taking the initiative, which at least sometimes relieves his boss of the responsibility of personal involvement.

Although most managers prefer not to work for this type, a capable Dictator is sometimes preferred over other types of leaders. One executive expressed it this way:

Sure he drives us, but at least you know where you stand, there's no mealy-mouthing around about things. You know what you're supposed to do. And another thing, he supports his men. You do a good job, and he'll take care of you. If you don't, you're on the outside looking in.

The Opportunist

The Opportunist is described in number 3.[11] He is usually intelligent and at least superficially personable. He is almost completely self-oriented, and results attained for the company are in his own best interests. In extreme examples, his ethics may be questionable. He is often quite adept and consequently pro-motable.

The Opportunist is found at the third and higher levels of management. He is in the lower levels, too, but is more difficult to detect there since his opportunism must be disguised if he is to survive. Those who display an appreciable amount of opportunism at the lower levels are usually separated from the company, both as a result of detection by higher management and by failure to get the desired results from their people who tend to oppose their efforts. Consequently, the Opportunists who survive the lower levels are the more perceptive and adept individuals. At the third and higher levels, the Opportunist usually progresses as rapidly as the Executives, Dictators, and Noncontroversial Conformists.

The Opportunist tends to select management people for his organization who are also Opportunists and perhaps more im-portantly to elicit opportunistic tendencies in those who under other types of supervision show little tendency in this direction. These people are *required* to become more opportunistic to meet the demands of the organization and even to survive, as illustrated by the following comments:

> I normally don't believe in cutting corners and never did, but I didn't have any choice. This job's competitive, and I want to get ahead just as much as the next guy. It becomes a question of doing what everybody else is doing or getting in trouble over production. Most of the regional sales managers were forcing our distributors to accept excess inventories so they could show increased sales, at least on paper. I wouldn't do it for a while and then had to make a decision to either do it or take a chance on my career. O.K., so I did it, but once I made up my mind, I did it right. I got tricky as hell. I even managed to unload outside my territory and made sure it didn't happen to me. And what happens? I get promoted. If you think I'm proud of it, you're mistaken, though. I don't even like to think of it. I didn't do anything dishonest, but maybe it stretched ethics more than a little. I haven't done anything like that since. Haven't had to, and hope to hell I never have to again.

The manager in the above example feels that he was a victim of circumstances—faced with unethical company expectations on one side and his own aversion to such methods on the other. This appears quite common when a segment of management is faced with extreme opportunism by a higher-level executive, regardless of the levels of supervision above the Opportunist.

The Opportunist often escapes detection due to his own abilities and the tendency in some companies to disbelieve the existence of opportunism.

> Jim, the executive vice president, said he'd heard stories about . . . [the Opportunist], but he couldn't see any justification for them, no proof at all. He thought it was sour grapes because . . . [the Opportunist] got better results. And, of course, I was sitting there doctoring production reports day in and day out just to keep on the payroll. He made us do it, though of course he didn't tell us to openly. If I didn't have a wife and kids I'd have told Jim, let him see what he thought about that. But I can't, around here we all play ostrich just to keep a little self-respect. It's a hell of a way to run a business. . . . [The Opportunist] will get a big fat promotion before too long and maybe we'll be out of it. I pity his replacement. If he plays it straight, he will have to somehow justify his lower production. That's one job I sure don't want.

The preceding is a case of extreme opportunism which creates not only an untenable position for the nonopportunists, but can and often does create a problem for the Opportunist's successor. There are varying degrees of opportunism, many not nearly as radical as this.

The Opportunist's proclivity for self-perpetuation is evident in these comments:

> Bill has been in trouble off and on ever since he quit working for . . . [the Opportunist]. He was held back a time or two, and almost fired the way I hear it. Then . . . [the Opportunist] comes back at a higher level and first thing you know Bill starts getting promoted again, bang, bang, bang, and now he's the number two man. Figure that one out.

Opportunism is as with other things a matter of degree, and there may be some in most people. Nevertheless, those individuals so classified by their supervisors and peers are as promotable in many firms at the third and higher levels as those in any other classification. The extreme examples always run the risk of total detection, however, and the possibility of ended careers is perhaps somewhat greater than in other classifications. This is difficult to substantiate since there is a reluctance to give real reasons for resignations within upper-management levels.

As with the Dictators, some people would rather work for a "mild Opportunist" than for an extreme "puritan." As one executive put it, "Sure, he may be looking out for himself some, but who isn't? At least we don't have to inventory the paper clips before we leave every night, and listen to those lectures on honesty is the best policy, mother love, and God knows what else."

The Noncontroversial Conformist

Response number 4 indicates a Noncontroversial Conformist.[12] He is a friendly, likable, conforming, warm, intelligent, socially adept individual. He does not crusade for better management and often gets credit for abilities he doesn't always use or perhaps possess. He seldom sticks his neck out and consequently stays out of trouble. People normally like to work for him since he lets them produce. Consequently, he is usually successful as a manager. He is often highly promotable.

This classification is appropriate for a large percentage of upper-management people, especially in those large firms with less than almost total objectivity.[13] The following quotation was obtained by following up a casual remark with a series of *why's.*

I'm glad [the Noncontroversial Conformist] got that position.

Why?

Well, he's a good man. I'm really impressed with him, always have been. I think he's capable.

Why?

Well, I don't know. I just like him. I think he knows how to go about things.

Why?

Well, he just does. I've seen him operate, handle people, solve problems. I was in a conference with him, and he got everybody's opinion and figured out what to do. And everybody was pleased.

Why?

They like him, everybody does. He stays calm and collected and is considerate of everybody and doesn't have an enemy in this company.

Why?

Well, he doesn't do anything to upset anybody.

Why?

What do you mean why? He just doesn't. Doesn't operate that way. I don't know him too well of course . . .

Why?

I've been around him quite a bit, but I'm not really too close to him, don't know anybody who is . . .

Why?

I hadn't thought about it, but I don't know who his really close friends are, or if he has any. He may not, come to think of it.

Why?

Well, he doesn't seem to get close to anybody specifically, just everybody generally. Everybody likes him, I know that.

Why?

I don't know. He doesn't do anything. People do it for him, I guess. Is that what you're getting at?

This informal interview was so easy to obtain when discussing a Noncontroversial Conformist that the above quotation applies almost equally to individuals in other companies, people in the same company, and to the same person with several interviewees.

The most notable consideration in discussing this classification is that those who admire the individual do so for very simple reasons of which they are generally unaware.

The same pattern applies in informal discussions following the remark, "I like Mr. So-and-So."

He's the nicest thing. Didn't know us except that we worked for the company, but came right over to our table in the company cafeteria and introduced himself and talked awhile. He's the greatest. All the girls like him.

Well, he came down on the line, just leaned back on a lathe and chatted with the men, let them know he knew how they were working, let them know he appreciated it without saying so. Didn't make a speech, just talked awhile. Most of the brass won't do that.

The Noncontroversial Conformist is promotable, sometimes highly so, in many organizations. His career is seldom in jeopardy since he usually does little that will offend anybody. People normally like to work for him since he lets them produce.

He's easier to work for than my previous supervisors. He doesn't go around ramming something down your throat all the time, telling you how to do every little thing. Makes you want to do a good job to please him, and lets you alone to do it. I like him because he respects me as a person.

The Executive

The manager who fits in the fifth classification is the Executive. His self-interest is constructive, and he is sincerely interested in the company. He is not a Dictator or Opportunist and may resemble a Noncontroversial Conformist except that he does something. He is the most successful and productive manager.[8] He usually displays a flexible approach designed to meet the requirements of the specific conditions.

The Executive has a flexible leadership style. He considers the most appropriate managerial approach under given circumstances, the employees to whom it is directed, and appropriate timing. He relies on democratic methods but reserves the final decision for himself. He works through motivated people and promotes conditions that integrate high productivity and high morale through team action.[9]

There are varying degrees of ability within any classification. For example, a Technician or a Dictator may be highly skilled or they may have lesser talents. A highly skilled Dictator may be more effective than an average Executive.

An Executive may act as a Dictator for a temporary period if the condition requires this approach. He will sometimes initially take a dictatorial approach when assigned to an operation requiring immediate correction. After correction, he reverts to more democratic methods.

The Executive is almost always a 3 on the Actual Balance scale. His self-interest, that is, his drive for achievement and recognition is constructive and is, therefore, related to company interest.

The Dictators (and Opportunists and Noncontroversial Conformists) would be appreciably more effective if they could develop the perspective of the Executive. He uses a democratic approach, but still functions as the leader,[10] as shown by the following comment:

> Just about everybody respects Ayers, and I don't know anyone who wouldn't willingly work for him. I think that basically he is a fine person, and he is capable. He leads his people rather than drives them, and I think he is truly interested in doing the best he can for the company. He expects everyone to do his best, but he respects people.

In addition to these classifications of promotables, there are three other classifications which must be mentioned but were not covered in the classification form.

The Abdicator

The Abdicator has either been defeated by the organization and consequently does as little as possible or abdicates, due to interest in outside activities or business interests. These reasons may or may not be related.

Those individuals who take a "free ride" at the expense of the company due to self-interest or an almost total lack of company interest are considered as Opportunists rather than as Abdicators for our purposes. Abdicators, of course, are rarely promotable.

The Manipulator

The Manipulator is a breed of executive who is highly skilled in the art of using mergers and acquisitions to build huge corporations or conglomerates. Their major interest lies not in the actual problems of managing such an enterprise, but in the chase—the willingness to take tremendous risks. Men such as Tex Thornton and Jim Ling fit this portrait of the new executive. These men, of course, are outside the scope of our research since we concentrated on the promotables within the firm. Manipulators are the top executives of business empires.

The Incompetent

Some individuals are basically incompetent for various reasons, such as insufficient intelligence, ill health, or age. These non-promotables are readily recognized and consequently are not discussed in detail.

Most managers were easily classified by their peers and by knowledgeable executives within the organization. This was usually done without hesitation. Nevertheless, as with any system of general classification, there were some who did not fit readily into a classification since there is always some degree of overlap. For example, one person was classified as an Executive with Noncontroversial Conformist, Dictator, and even Abdicator tendencies depending on circumstances. This was one of the most extreme cases encountered and the individual was classified as an Executive since he displayed these tendencies more than the others.

Literature Cited

1. Powell, p. 60.

2. McFarland puts it this way, "Individuals . . . often are surprised to learn that honesty, sincerity, energy, enthusiasm, and above-average mentality are not the assets they thought. . . . Not infrequently the person indifferent

to these values rises higher than the one who strictly adheres to them. This can be disillusioning and frustrating." Dalton E. McFarland, *Management: Principles and Practices*, 2nd ed. (New York: The MacMillan Company, 1964), pp. 439-440.

3. Lyman W. Porter and Edward E. Lawler III, *Managerial Attitudes and Performance*, p. 118.

4. See Aaron Levenstein, *Why People Work* (New York: Collier Books, 1964), p. 32.

5. William H. Whyte, Jr., *The Organization Man* (New York: Doubleday and Company, Inc., 1956).

6. Robert Sheenan, "Montgomery Ward—Prosperity Is Still Around the Corner," *Management: Challenge and Response, Readings from Fortune*, eds. Charter, Weintraub, and Ray (New York: Holt, Rinehart, and Winston, 1965), pp. 101-112.

7. Sheenan, pp. 112-124.

8. See R. H. Guest, *Organizational Change: The Effect of Successful Leadership* (Homewood, Illinois: Dorsey, 1962), pp. 40-81.

9. Ibid.

10. Daniel Katz and Robert L. Kahn, *The Social Psychology of Organizations* (New York: John Wiley and Sons, Inc., 1966), pp. 325-327.

11. Ernest Dale reports on some of the activities of Opportunists in *Planning and Developing the Company Organization Structure* (New York: American Management Association, Research Report No. 20, 1952), p. 88. Also see Marshall E. Dimock, *The Executive in Action* (New York: Harper and Brothers, 1945), pp. 65-66, for a discussion of power relationships concerning politics in organizations.

12. F. A. Shull, "Administrative Perspectives of Human Relations," *Advanced Management*, XXV (March, 1960), 18-22.

13. See Robert R. Blake and Jane S. Mouton, *The Managerial Grid* (Houston: Gulf Publishing Company, 1964), pp. 134-136.

3 : the promotables
and their battlegrounds

This chapter presents a description of the companies researched as well as an analysis of the promotable managers and their methods. Subsequent chapters will build upon the background material presented here.

Wildcat Petroleum, Inc.

Wildcat* is a large independent petroleum company which operated as a partnership just prior to and during the Ranger, Texas oil boom beginning in 1917 with the John McCleskey discovery-well just south of the city. One of the original partners, Karl Schmidt, is president of the company, but the company is controlled by the chairman of the board of directors, John Keeton.

This firm was selected since it was originally a vigorous growth company created by the hard work, initiative, and foresight of its founders. But it is now a nongrowth company expecting absorption by some major oil company. This investigation reveals the evolution from high objectivity to its present low objectivity and the high self-interest now shown by many members of upper management.

---

*The identity of this company (as well as the identity of other companies researched and names of all individuals involved) has been disguised to protect the anonymity of the company and managers who so freely contributed to this study.

Wildcat was created through drilling and leasing operations during the Ranger, Texas oil boom, principally in the Hogtown area southeast of Ranger. Its headquarters is now located in a distant major city, and it is the organization of the headquarters which is considered in this study. A portion of the organization chart is shown in Figure 3-1.

Figure 3-1. Partial Organization Chart—Wildcat Petroleum, Inc.

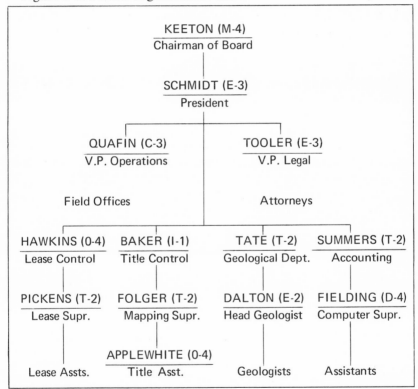

The organization chart shown in Figure 3-1 will be used throughout the study for reference to the organizational structure and the management team. The coding following each name indicates the classification for each individual and the rating on the Actual Balance scale.

Keeton, chairman of the board of directors, is shown as an M-4—a Manipulator with almost total self-interest. Schmidt is an E-3, an Executive with almost a balance between self-interest and company interest, as is Tooler, vice president legal, and Dalton, the head geologist. Quafin, vice president-operations, is a Non-controversial Conformist, and Hawkins and Applewhite are both Opportunists with high self-interest.

Fielding is a Dictator with high self-interest, and four individuals are Technicians with more company interest than self-interest. Baker is a company-oriented Incompetent. A number of other individuals are not identified since identification is not necessary for the study.

The background is presented in a large part through statements such as the following by Tooler:

> This place is dead. It died at least ten years ago when Jake passed away and Schmidt lost control. We haven't done much since but ride herd on our properties and handle a few leases. The Old Man tried to keep things going, but Keeton and the board wouldn't let him—not interested in anything except protecting their investment.
>
> The Old Man fought them for awhile, but it wasn't any use, and we both knew it. I told him we'd just better make the best of things the way they are and not drive ourselves nuts. He knew it wasn't any use.
>
> He is still watching, though. He'd still run this outfit if Keeton gave him half a chance. There's still money to be made in oil—lots of it—and the Old Man knows how. We still have plenty to do, but it's not like it used to be—exciting and always something going on, never knowing from one day to the next whether we'd hit a big one or lose our shirts.

Schmidt, president of the company, recalled the events which preceded the founding of the company:

> Hell, me and old Jake used to run this company. Started it back in Burkburnett. Had an old wore-out string of tools, and was drilling down about 2,000 feet knowing it'd come up dry or a low producer, when another driller came by with a Wichita Falls paper over a week old. Said they brought in a gusher at Ranger. I wasn't much more than a kid, but

we'd been around long enough to know what it most likely meant. We started loading right then. Didn't say "Hello," "Goodby," "Kiss my foot," or nothing–just pulled up and loaded our string and left out. Headed for Ranger.

Tooler, vice president-legal, discussed the sale of company properties:

Quafin's O.K. and does what he can. He's the other V.P., and he takes care of what production we've got. It seems to me he spends most of his time closing down the field operations and selling off what equipment we have left. He sold the last of our company houses at the camps some time back. We're just about a paper company now–very little equipment left.

The only real operation we've got's in leasing. Hawkins runs it, such as it is. I don't know how we stay in business. He got the wrong block and section number a couple years back and dropped fifty thousand on the wrong lease.

He seems to do O.K. though, since he knows the guys in the other independents and some of the majors. He probably gets as much out of them as he does from Geological [Tate]. Hawkins looks out for himself, too, and picks up a good one on the side once in awhile.

Folger, the mapping supervisor, discussed Applewhite, his assistant, by stating:

I handle the mapping, mostly, and have Applewhite to help, but he does everything else but, it seems. He believes in being seen, and is always over jawing with Hawkins and into something all the time. I can't do anything with him since Baker [title control] ignores it. Applewhite wants in leasing with Hawkins, but there's no room for him unless they move Pickens out, and Pickens does most of the work over there. Pickens is getting tired of Applewhite. I'm glad he wants in over there instead of my job. I'd settle him down, except he knows everybody around here and is always doing something for somebody, except me.

Schmidt viewed Applewhite, an Opportunist, in a different light:

That kid's always in something. Anytime I want something special done, up he pops like a jack-in-a-box. That boy gets around. Some of them wonder why I don't have Baker get rid of him. Don't understand it. Maybe think I ain't quite bright. Hell, I know what that boy's up to. Wants in leasing. Wants Pickens' job, most likely. Not going to get it though. Pickens is a good man—solid. Need him where he is. Do you know why I keep him around? Keeps everybody else awake—at least in there trying. Only trouble with that boy—he was born forty-fifty years too late. Should've been in Hogtown.

Amalgamated Electronics, Inc.

Amalgamated is a large, well-established firm with diversified products in the electronics field. It was chosen as a case study since it is an old company but is now experiencing unprecedented growth, due in part to recent product superiority in certain segments of its field.

Amalgamated has over 70,000 employees in plants throughout the United States, as well as some foreign investments. Our study covers one major plant facility with over 4,000 employees. Because of its age, size, and field of endeavor, Amalgamated has become bureaucratic and operates on limited decentralization with sharing of authority and decision-making at the upper levels and a somewhat regimented operation at the lower levels of supervision.

The portion of the organization chart shown in Figure 3-2 covers a period of several years. More than one name is shown for some positions, indicating the order in which individuals held a given position.

There is a great deal of movement between plant facilities and to and from the company headquarters, which has a large staff. The opening of a new plant necessitates transfer of trained people for the nucleus of the new management team. Consequently, opportunities for promotion are much greater than in industry as a whole.

This firm has medium objectivity.

The portion of the organization chart shown in Figure 3-2 indicates that Hill, a Dictator with almost complete self-interest, was general plant manager at the beginning of the period under

Figure 3-2.
Partial Organization Chart—Amalgamated Electronics, Inc.

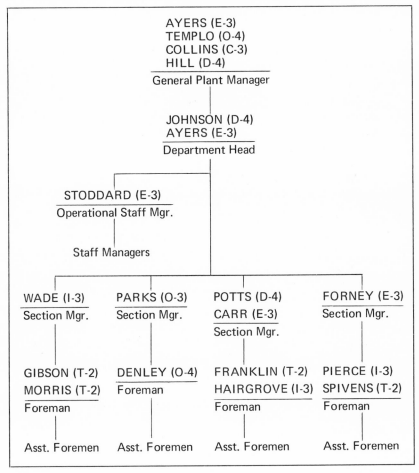

study. He was replaced by Collins, a Noncontroversial Conformist with almost a balance between self-interest and company interest. Collins, in turn, was replaced by Templo, a self-oriented Opportunist, followed by Ayers, an Executive who prior to this was the department head.

For simplicity, not all movement for the period was shown at levels below the general plant manager. Other classifications and

Actual Balances shown include Incompetents and Technicians varying from 2's with more company interest than self-interest, to 3's with almost a balance. The 1's in this case are in the assistant-foremen ranks and are not identified.

Hill, when general plant manager, discussed his operational philosophy:

> As head of this plant, I'm in competition with the heads of our other plants. I'm older than most of them, but I have enough time left to have a chance at the operational v.p. job, though I know that the presidency is impossible since I'm older than he is. The only way I have to further my career is to compete—do a better job, get better overall results and recognition for those results. That's how I got where I am in the first place, digging in and doing what has to be done.

> The only way to get those results is to build a management team capable of producing them. This means getting the best possible people and training them, developing them to have the capabilities for the job, laying out what is expected, and showing them how to do it. This business is complicated, and it takes top managers, people who are aggressive and want to do the job.

> I keep my door open—let my people communicate with me, and I communicate with them. We have the organizational hierarchy, sure, but I paddle my boat right around it anytime I feel like it. I call a foreman or drop in unannounced anytime I see the need for it. If he's not doing the job, he hears from me. The men know it, too—keeps 'em alert, keeps 'em hungry, and I want them to be. I spend a lot of time down on the line. That way I know what's going on—who's doing what. Maybe I won't move off this job ever, but I'll have a good tight operation—one everybody in this plant can take pride in.

Ayers, when department head, was not in complete agreement with his supervisor's philosophy:

> I wish to hell Hill wouldn't keep going around me tearing up the men. He came down and crawled Morris [foreman] but good, and I had to patch it up with Wade, one of our section managers, and get Morris settled down so we could get the line rolling again. Morris had nothing to do with it—only been in his job a couple of weeks. The problem's in

maintenance, anyway. Sure it helps to give them a pat on the back now and again, but a boot in the britches doesn't help if they don't need jacked up. Wade should be the one to do it, anyhow.

Wade, the section manager, was unsuccessful in his mild attempt at protecting his employee:

> Well sir, I just stood there and let him ream Morris—wasn't anything else I could do. I tried to explain that Morris was new, but Hill had a handful of production reports, and he wouldn't listen—gave me one of those looks. Now Morris is upset with me as if it's my fault. He's got to learn to take care of himself like everybody else. There's nothing I can do. I told him, forget it, get the line moving, and next time Hill will be bragging on him.

Carr, another section manager, gave these observations concerning the situation:

> That Wade kills me. He could have spoken up for Morris. Hill doesn't come down here chewing on Hairgrove, and he needs it if anybody does. Hill respects you more if you stand up to him, providing you're right. I just tell him what the score is. Ayers acts as a buffer as much as he can, but his hands are tied sometimes. If Hill knew how much Ayers softens some of his edicts, he'd have a fit. We do get the job done though, what with Hill pushing all the time and Ayers taking it a little easier.

> We're ahead of the other plants most of the time. I'd rather have it this way than the way it is at . . . [another plant]. I call Stevens the first of the month after the reports are out and rib hell out of him. Guys move faster here, too.

Morris was not at all pleased with his introduction to Hill's operational philosophy:

> O.K., so I got reamed right off, but I'm learning. The guys said Wade wouldn't take care of you, so now I know. I don't think he really knew what to do, so I'm not sore at him. I just wish I worked for Carr or Forney, maybe even Parks. Hell of a promotion this is going to turn out to be.

Diversified Manufacturing, Inc.

Diversified is a national manufacturing company with assets approaching the one billion mark. The company manufactures a number of products in widely divergent fields. Our investigation covers a major plant facility with an appreciable capital investment. The plant employs about 500 highly skilled people. This plant was selected since under previous top management it had considerably less corporate objectivity than it has under its present management. The plant now has almost total objectivity.

A partial organization chart is shown in Figure 3-3.

Figure 3-3.
Partial Organization Chart–Diversified Manufacturing, Inc.

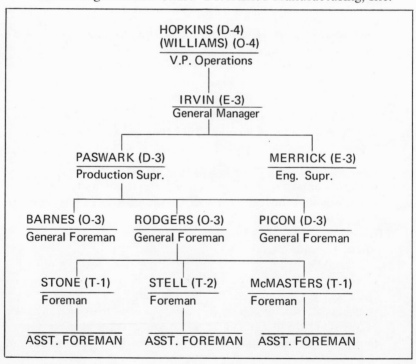

McMasters, a foreman, commented on the change in operations which resulted from the appointment of Hopkins as vice president of operations:

> This place sure has changed since Hopkins took over. Stone and I both like it a lot better, even though things are really tougher for us foremen. Not tougher, really, not since we got things straightened out. I mean this plant is operating properly now, which actually makes it easier after you get over the hump.

Stone verified McMasters's comments:

> I don't think Williams cared about the plant. He didn't spend all his time here like Hopkins does, and everything went to pot—just no organization. McMasters and I work together now—make sure inventories are in shape for each other. And Rodgers is able to help us more—let us pull together, sort of.

Irvin commented on the previous top executive in the plant facility:

> Being general manager under a boss like Williams is an experience I won't soon forget. I never knew what to do. Communications broke down between us and the parent company—that sort of thing. I did what I could, but I admit I couldn't control it and couldn't keep things organized properly. Just little things would get us balled up. Williams didn't seem concerned, and I guess I wouldn't either if I had all the money he has—loaded like that. But hell, if he's going to work, he might as well work, or quit like he finally did. Wish he'd done it sooner. Now with Hopkins we're getting along fine. Everybody's reasonably happy, and we look good.

Diversified had been experiencing considerable difficulty under the plant's previous top executive, Williams (although he resigned prior to our study, we were generally familiar with the operation under his management). The objectivity of the plant, as well as general morale, was low and the management team seemed to be floundering with little sense of direction. There was an immediate improvement with Hopkins' assumption of command, however, and objectivity and employee morale rose appreciably.

Stell summarizes the attitude of some of the plant's first-level supervisors toward their top executive:

> Hopkins is O.K. for my money. He really has the interests of the company at heart. Being foreman under him is really a pleasure. Gives me lots of job satisfaction—a feeling of accomplishment. The guy's plenty smart—knows everything that goes on here, pushes to get things done right, and we're well-organized.

Although the lower-level managers had worked under the previous operations vice president, they had limited company experience. This inexperience and their naiveté superficially gave the impression that any person would be fortunate to be a part of the organization. The high degree of company interest did not necessarily contribute to the most desirable working conditions, however, as we will observe later.

The formal organization charts of the three firms—Wildcat, Amalgamated, and Diversified—present the official relationships within the companies. These relationships, in the reality of organizational life, are often circumvented or changed by the informal actions within the corporate subculture. Yet, these formal blueprints do serve as basic background and as a point of departure into the corporate subculture.

4 : life in the corporate subculture

Our American society consists of a number of subsocieties, and the most important to many adults is the corporate subculture. Professional, social, and interpersonal relationships make up the specific subculture of the company, and these are important organizational assets.

As with any culture, there are mores and taboos and rules of conduct—both written and unwritten, formal and informal. The company philosophy or climate reflects the *group* philosophies of its people and changes as the people move in and out and within the company.[1] The result is a very complex and volatile culture through whose myriad mazes the employee must find his way.

The subcultures vary from company to company, and yet are very much the same. All require degrees of conformity both to formal organizational expectancies and to the informal group. Certainly companies exert profound influences on their people, and with the mobility of the population, the company's evaluation of the worth of the individual not only determines his economic status, but his geographic location.

Organizations, out of necessity, exert considerable control over employees with managers both controlling and being controlled. The price paid for membership in the culture is acceptance of partial control of one's destiny,[2] and the price paid for controlling others rests with the individual. Determining who will or will not receive a raise or a promotion, who will be hired or fired, who will be transferred to a distant and, to the person, perhaps foreign location are responsibilities met within the framework of company policy and the objective-subjective analyses of the person or group of persons with whom the decisions rest.

A manager willingly accepts such restrictions on his freedom mainly because he is a social animal, a gregarious creature who survives only in the midst of others of his kind. Certainly many individuals are capable of surviving economically outside their companies, yet few have a burning desire to leave their corporate subcultures even when this may be wise.

Why employees wish to stay within a company is an involved and complicated problem. Although some employees may not fully recognize it and may rationalize, the compelling reason in most cases is the individual's incapability of operating effectively outside his chosen subculture.

When a person measures his success, he is usually influenced by the opinions of his associates. He cares a great deal what his fellow employees think of him. A person who has left a firm for economic advantage is not necessarily admired since most people measure success within the framework of their own subculture.

The social relationships of most people revolve around others with whom they work. Friendships usually must include some sort of common interest or common tie. This is automatically provided for employees of the same company since they have the common interest of the company and common knowledge of company operations, activities, and interpersonal relationships. Social gatherings, whether formal or informal, attended by company employees invariably include discussions of company activities, a subject which is inexhaustible for the active members of the subculture, often to the dismay of wives or husbands who have never been employed by the company. Those who were previously employed by the company usually are capable of entering into such discussions with as much fervor and interest as the active members.

Companies often encourage the close personal relationships in an effort to create and maintain a healthy environment on the thesis that group activities by employees create loyalty to the company. This environment contributes to the solidarity of the subculture, which in turn requires the sacrifices by the individuals for membership.

Formal company-sponsored programs such as baseball teams, bowling leagues, and golf tournaments are designed for this purpose. Most progressive managers agree, however, that these programs, while contributing to a sound organization climate and group loyalty, may not be true individual motivators. On the other hand, these programs may *condition* the employee to accept motivators tied directly to their work—such as achievement, recognition, and advancement.[3]

As a consequence of the subculture, the employee becomes so enmeshed in his work in his subculture that he finds it difficult or even completely undesirable to extricate himself, even if he wishes. The corporate subculture is the focal point around which almost all managers—the organization men—of large companies revolve. It is the rewards given and the punishments exacted, as well as the conduct and capabilities of the individual, which determine the effectiveness of his adjustment to his company.

The Corporate Subculture of Wildcat

Wildcat's corporate subculture, while similar in many respects to Amalgamated and Diversified's, is so different in other respects that it defies comparison. As a nongrowth company, openings occur infrequently—as the result of resignations and retirements. The question of promotability is of little interest to the employees. Transfers occur rarely.

The employees feel varying degrees of loyalty to the firm, depending on the length of service. The *big-family* effect exists to a lesser degree than in Amalgamated and Diversified and is created by the unavoidable interpersonal relationship of the employees rather than by any planned company effort.

To understand the corporate subculture of Wildcat, one is forced to consider not the present or the future, as with Amalgamated and Diversified, but the past, for what Wildcat is and will become is of secondary importance to its older employees. The loyalty to the firm and the interpersonal relationships among its employees, the feeling of kinship shown by those who work for a common cause, is irrevocably tied to the past.

The archives in Amalgamated and Diversified are viewed by the employees as boxes of records in a storeroom, but at Wildcat the archives in a basement vault of the headquarters building are viewed with respect, for here lies the proof of the once greatness of the company.

Schmidt, the president, who is above normal retirement age, constantly reminisces about the firm:

> That Ranger was really something, the boomingest boom there'd ever been. Time me and Jake got there, it was like a Saturday at the county fair. Seemed like everybody in the country was there or on the way. Didn't amount to much before—nice little town—but they was already throwing up buildings downtown and shacks all over. Had the whole place leased to start with, so we just contracted for our rig and started drilling. Couldn't of drilled ourselves anyway, cost twenty-five, thirty thousand, which was twenty-five, thirty more'n we had.

> People was getting rich overnight. Go to sleep broke and wake up rich. And plenty there to relieve them of it. Had drillers, tooldressers, roustabouts, lease men, speculators and everything else, including the real toughs. Started killing each other right off. Booze was flowing in shanty bars with the usual women. Some was buying leases left and right with money they didn't have and hitting it right so's they'd turn up rich. Hell, within a year there was thirty thousand people there all for the same reason—money—same as me and Jake.

The employees' concern for money is more moderately expressed in this observation:

> One thing we all have in common here is the quick and speculative glance we all take at our paychecks on payday. We have no formalized intervals or amounts for raises and no formalized employee-appraisal routines. As a result, we never know when to anticipate a salary adjustment. The automatic analysis of the gross amount of our checks has become a reflex.

With promotions improbable and wage adjustments uncertain, the self-interest of the employee is sometimes directed to outside interests, such as in the case of Hawkins (in charge of the leasing operations) who "picks up a good one [lease] on the side once in awhile."

Applewhite's interest in a transfer is also somewhat self-oriented:

> I'd like to get in leasing with Hawkins if I could do it. I think the work would be more stimulating, and I'd learn more about the business—something that I could use to my own advantage, perhaps. Hawkins probably makes as much picking up a few leases as he gets here, although I realize there is some risk involved.

Others react to the lack of opportunities by showing less concern for the business. Folger says:

> I do what has to be done and see that it is done right, and I don't question what is given to me to do. That's not my problem. I get the drafting done, and then I go home and forget it. I used to take more interest in it maybe, but now I don't question anything. They want block and section maps. They get them. They want me to plat the moon, I guess I'd do that too—to scale.

But through any discussion with the employees, run the threads of the past:

> Jake figured the thing to do was to keep drilling until we had a big enough stake and then do our own leasing. They was starting to bring some wells in on farther out—independents and some of the majors. And the field kept expanding, so we was working, watching and waiting, and figuring to get in on some of the really big money sooner or later. That was before Hogtown came in, before we went to Hogtown.

The Corporate Subculture of Amalgamated

Amalgamated's subculture is typical of those of large businesses and in many respects is similar to Diversified's. The employees are for the most part devoted to the firm and consider it a "good place to work." Comments such as, "I like it here," and "Most of my friends work here" are common.

The firm has a somewhat benevolent attitude toward its employees. It considers the needs and desires of its people, and, within the limits ·imposed by the requirements of the business, attempts to treat its employees with fairness and respect. This is a sincere interest in the welfare of the employees, and not a paternalistic approach.

Determination of what is in the employee's best interests is based on the general philosophy of the company which prides itself on equitable treatment. Since Amalgamated is a growth company and consequently needs experienced people for newly constructed plants, a major requirement for promotability is mobility. Amalgamated has no reluctance in moving people throughout the United States at frequent intervals. A prerequisite for direct employment into the management ranks and in some production levels is a willingness to move to other geographic areas at the discretion of the company. Such moves provide the experience and product knowledge required for promotability to higher levels of management. This is, of course, also true of most large companies, including Diversified.

The interpretation of the company's philosophy in relation to its employees is the responsibility of the individual manager, and, as a result, there is some variance between sections and between managers. The classification of the manager influences the expectancy of those under his supervision. A Technician usually expects his employees to be loyal, hard working, and company oriented and may insist that they meet these requirements or give the appearance of doing so. A Dictator demands obedience and results, while Opportunists, depending on their degree of opportunism, may require opportunistic tendencies by their people. These general managerial approaches in Amalgamated affect the company-employee relationship.

More specifically, a manager's personal philosophy, as well as the company's general philosophy, may have a profound influence on a manager's employees. Social drinking is informally encouraged in Amalgamated, as is conformity to society in general and the business society specifically. Drunkenness is discouraged and can result in disciplinary action. Some managers are opposed to drinking on moral or religious grounds and may exert pressures, possibly unspoken, on their employees in this respect.

There are similar demands of an unlimited variety, depending on the philosophy of the manager. Consequently, the management employees of Amalgamated must not only conform to company expectations but also to the expectations of their supervisors. This flexibility of adjustment is an important factor in promotability, although the managers do not consider it formally and may not consciously recognize its existence.

Concern for employees varies considerably among the managers. Consequently, Amalgamated's general benevolent consideration of its employees is in opposition to its callousness in specific instances.

Amalgamated's corporate subculture closely resembles that of other major businesses, with emphasis on the corporate family, loyalty to the welfare of the company, and some regard for its people. Most management employees with at least a few years service are enmeshed in the subculture and the assumed security it offers. Their professional, social, and personal lives cannot be viewed except within the context of the company.

The Corporate Subculture of Diversified

Diversified's corporate subculture closely resembles that of Amalgamated, but since this company has a higher degree of company interest, there are differences.

As a result of the top executive's operational philosophy, there is a high degree of objectivity at all levels of management. The employees believe that the only way to earn promotions and raises is with ability and performance, and that social or personal relationships have no bearing on promotability. We found these beliefs to be valid. This is possibly the most significant difference between Diversified and Amalgamated since these relationships importantly affect promotability in Amalgamated.

The emphasis on job performance at Diversified diminishes the concern for conformity to standards of dress and speech. In addition, promotability is generally considered in relation to the employee's ability to perform at the next level of supervision rather than in terms of total potential for advancement.

Diversified, like Amalgamated, encourages a family atmosphere among its employees and sponsors athletic activities and some social affairs. There is a great deal of loyalty to the company, and social and personal relationships usually involve fellow employees. Unlike Amalgamated, however, there is somewhat less reluctance for managers to leave the company. More employees resign to accept higher-paying positions than is the case at Amalgamated. This is due, in part, to special technical skills which are learned at Diversified and are in demand by other businesses.

The employee's immediate supervisor at Diversified, as well as at Wildcat and Amalgamated, exercises a considerable amount of control over the employee's future. "He can't necessarily get you promoted," the saying goes, "but he can darn sure get you fired." Even in this overly simplified form, this statement reflects one of the most important aspects of an employee's adjustment to his organization: the supervisor-employee relationship.

At Diversified, as well as at any company, the employee has three obligations: (1) to his company, (2) to himself, and (3) to his supervisor. He theoretically owes his company his loyalty and best efforts. He owes himself consideration for his own general welfare. He owes his boss his loyalty.

At Diversified, all employees are expected to consider their supervisor's welfare, as well as their own, and this principally means not getting him in trouble. An employee normally can survive his own errors if these do not embarrass his supervisor or cause an adverse effect on his supervisor's career. If they do, however, the employee's career may be in jeopardy. Recognition of this unwritten and unexplained condition is a factor in the employee's adjustment to the company.

The secrecy in handling personnel movement at Diversified is sometimes carried to extremes. Most advancements cause others, resulting in a series of moves at the various levels, as is often true in any large business. Since a change in planned movement at any level can result in altered plans at lower or even higher levels, such personnel adjustments remain unannounced until the series of moves are imminent.

The employees are considered only to the degree that company interests are not impaired. Consequently, employees make major investments, such as buying new homes, or making major renovations, or similar, more personal decisions without being advised that a transfer to a distant location is planned. To what degree such information is given informally is unknown, but it appears the exception rather than the rule since supervisors consider such action risky.

The supervisor is also the most influential person in arranging wage adjustments and promotions. It is true in most cases that he can end an employee's career. While he may not be able to control the promotability of his employees, his active participation is almost always required. Therefore, not only the company controls the destiny of the individual, but the immediate supervisor, as the representative of the company and appraiser of the individual, exercises almost unlimited control.

Diversified's operational philosophy is created almost entirely by the head of the plant. Hopkins is a Dictator with almost total self-interest, but this self-interest is directed, as with all Dictators, toward obtaining results. This personal philosophy permeates the subculture, and the subculture is an extension of this dominating personality.

Literature Cited

1. Keith Davis, *Human Relations at Work: The Dynamics of Organizational Behavior*, 3rd ed. (New York: McGraw-Hill Book Company, 1967), p. 81.

2. Francis E. Merril, *Society and Culture* (Englewood Cliffs, New Jersey: Prentice-Hall, Inc., 1965), p. 508.

3. See Scott Meyers, "Who Are Your Motivated People," *Harvard Business Review*, XLII (January-February, 1964), 73-88.

5 : how the informal organization works

Informal considerations within the organization often have as much or more effect on the organization than the stated or formal directives and policies. We will consider such factors as official and unofficial actions, the personal image, horizontal and vertical cliques, adoptive nepotism and socionepotism, the grapevine, the corporate image, and executive isolation.

Official and Unofficial Actions

In the companies we studied, the official or stated policy or instructions and the actual expectancy were sometimes conflicting. After some experience in the companies, employees were usually able to interpret actual meanings of directives from stated meanings, an almost indispensable skill for effective management.[1] The more experienced and more perceptive employees were quite adept at this, but those with limited experience or perception were often bewildered.

In bureaucratic organizations such as Wildcat, Amalgamated, and Diversified, interpreting actual expectations is a daily necessity. The company's size and degree of bureaucracy, however, are directly related to the need for these interpretations.

The extent of these conflicting instructions can be determined by examining the volumes of correspondence covering instructions and information which normally originate at higher levels and are transmitted through the descending levels of the organization.

If the person responsible at each succeeding lower level agrees with the instructions, the stated and actual instructions are the same. If he does not agree and wants to modify the instructions, he must either do so openly or must veil his intentions. An open and straight-forward modification can be interpreted by those at higher levels as failure to carry out directives; but veiled modifications, if handled astutely, are difficult or impossible to detect. The manager often elects to veil his modifications, as can be seen in the following example at Amalgamated:

We received the instructions for the new panel assembly which were originated in the home office. They are too far away from our local operations to understand some basic problems, so some of it which is sound in theory just won't work here. Of course, there are some slightly different assembly procedures which are involved.

The cover letter with the instructions had been rewritten at some level, possibly more than one; and, although it was probably similar, its emphasis was on portions of the instructions which weren't emphasized in the actual instructions. It didn't say anything you could put your finger on, just suggested caution in certain phases of the assembly, but the intent was clear enough. It meant for us to follow the procedures which we know from experience are the most effective. This gets everybody off the hook except the foremen, but we're used to this.

It's not all that bad really, since higher management will usually protect us if it ever comes to that. This way everybody is happy, the panels are assembled properly and there's no fuss or bother. Except the foremen have to be able to read between the lines. If they don't, they could get in trouble on production.

Another technique used at Amalgamated involves de-emphasizing directives:

The cover letter said the instructions were attached, nothing more. If they feel strongly about anything, they write about it in the cover letter, so I know when I get one of these somebody isn't in full accord with it but can't or didn't make an issue of it. Where it's possible to do so, I disregard the instructions and usually I know what the divergence of opinion is all about and what I'm really expected to do. You learn after awhile.

A similar system is used at Amalgamated's lower levels to answer inquiries concerning some phase of the operation which is below standard.

> They want to know what's causing it and what we are doing to correct the condition. Sometimes you can tell the whole truth and sometimes you can't. The problem may be the result of something over which we have no control, possibly even a policy decision made by the official who's asking for the corrective analysis report. We learn in a hurry how to write the reports without really saying a thing, you know, describing the symptoms instead of the cause, and a bunch of high-sounding gibberish about how we're emphasizing zero defects and all that.

Most managers are aware that the day-to-day operations consist of negotiations and compromises[2]—that there is a need for "greasing the skids," "pump priming," and "plowing the field" before official action is taken.[3]

Several managers mentioned the psychological advantage in arranging for conferences or discussions with their peers to be held in their own offices so that they have the advantage of familiar surroundings while their *opponents* are on *foreign soil.* This also places the manager in a better position to control the discussion since he is usually behind the desk with the others facing him. He can automatically assume the role of leader. Some managers also use this technique in negotiating with their supervisors since discussions in an employee's office tend to be less formal.

These unofficial and semiofficial activities are effective within the limits of the skills of those participating. They involve interpersonal relationships, and the manager's effectiveness depends on his understanding of the operations within the subculture and his social adroitness in handling these situations.

In addition to the in-plant research, the authors surveyed a representative sample of *Fortune's* list of the largest 500 companies in the United States.* These companies were asked about various management practices, including the use of unofficial actions, cliques within their organizations, the use of the grapevine and so forth.

---

*See Appendix 2 for the Research Methodology.

The companies surveyed have a combined total of over 100,000 managerial personnel. These companies reported that 16 percent of their managers resorted to unofficial actions a great deal, while 75 percent did so frequently. Only 8 percent of these managers were reported to seldom use unofficial action, and no company said that their managers never use such methods. These companies considered unofficial practices a normal and necessary procedure. One executive of a major industrial empire commented: "This applies to all phases of the business, and we do this in an effort to prepare an individual for changes. This gives him an opportunity to begin to adjust his thinking, and he gradually makes himself a part of the consideration." Or perhaps, rephrased, recognizing and using unofficial methods helps the individual to adapt to his company's expectations—and to conform.

The Personal Image

Showmanship is often essential. That is, the image a person projects is often more important than his actual capabilities. It is the image, not the man, that is judged in terms of accomplishment and promotability.[4]

The personal image is formed in day-to-day activities and interpersonal relationships, both horizontally and vertically. The impression that a person makes on his peers and employees profoundly affects his supervisor's evaluations. Therefore, a person's career is affected, and sometimes his personal image is inconsistent with his capabilities.

Some men benefit by being judged on the basis of their image. For example, some men whose bearing is in keeping with the popular idea of the executive play the part. One man with Wildcat describes a fellow supervisor who is such a man:

> He has that distinguished look, the look of an executive: even features, graying at the temples, and erect carriage. And he acts the part, thoughtful and somewhat slow and reflective in his movements. He's polished of course, proper manners and grammatical speech, and he looks and acts like you expect an executive to act.

But when you really get to know him, you find out it's just a front, although it may be completely natural with him. I really thought he was extremely capable, just automatically assumed it I guess, until I got to know him quite well. The guy really borders on incompetency. . . . He's rather dull mentally, but if you suggested this to those who don't know him well, they would think you were out of your mind.*

The Noncontroversial Conformist is successful because of his personal image and his ability to create an environment conducive to individual production. This environment is due in part to his image, since it is the image he projects which makes him successful as a manager. That he seldom does anything himself, certainly nothing controversial, is almost never recognized by his associates and can only be explained as the result of people's credulity.

Promotions commonly affect the personal image. Promotions of managers, especially those who are not intimately known, are sometimes accompanied by the group conviction that the person possesses superior capabilities or intelligence solely on the basis of the promotions—a He-was-promoted-because-he-possesses-superior-ability-because-he-was-promoted type of *reasoning.*

This circular reasoning may also have the opposite result: those who aren't promoted are assumed to be less capable. This assumption may, of course, prevent advancement.

Something else that may affect the personal image is a man's area of specialization. The man who has always worked in one area is frequently assumed incapable of assignments outside his specialization. As a result, his assignments may be restricted.

The supervisor-employee relationship may provide a distorted view of the employee, a possibility seemingly overlooked by most managers even if they have experienced similar circumstances. The employee may be ill at ease with his immediate supervisor or one further removed, and the image projected under those circum-

---

*One owner of a large, successful executive placement agency which does in-depth testing, contends that about 10% of all executives are out and out frauds.

stances may be at considerable variance with the image projected under normal circumstances. One Diversified manager explained such a situation:

> Well, let's face it, he [his supervisor] scares hell out of me. I just can't relax with him, and sometimes I think he thinks I'm a stupid ass, which just makes it worse. He can't see me, obviously, unless he's there, so he never sees me as I really am, which really makes it tough. I've never had this trouble with any other boss, and I'm not the only one in this fix. He scares hell out of everybody.

In industry in general, there is a wide variance in the recognition and consideration of the effect of the personal image. Thirty percent of the largest firms report that they are completely aware of the importance of the personal image and consider it formally in employee appraisals. Forty percent consider it formally part of the time. Only twenty percent never consider it at all. Ten percent seem only vaguely aware of it.

Prudential considers the personal image important in investment and sales positions, although they recognize that this image may be at variance with the true self.

An executive of a manufacturing company which is completely aware of the importance of the personal image and considers it formally, summed up his feelings with one word, "People!"

An executive in the milling industry believes, "The image follows what a man actually is in a short time." No other executive shared his conviction.

A ranking corporate executive believes that the personal image can't be ignored since in some positions it seems to be of real and legitimate consequence. He hastens to point out, however, that in his company performance appraisals emphasize results, and salary increases are based on proven performance. Apparently in this company, objective employee analyses discount the recognized personal image.

The image projected by any individual as related to his company's expectations will determine his degree of promotability. Those who do adjust to their companies are at least informally aware of this. The importance of the image is shown by the allegation made by an employee at Amalgamated:

> I'll bet you I can end the career of any section head here by casually and repeatedly expressing sympathy for him to the other section heads every time some minor thing goes wrong and then waiting for it to come back to me to embellish and repeat again. Pretty soon it would get to higher management and they'd begin to wonder and watch. This sort of thing can happen here unintentionally by someone's talking too much. If I ever get vindictive and want to get even with someone, which I hope I never will, I'll do it just like that. The trouble is, it could happen to me just as easily.

Horizontal and Vertical Cliques

In all companies, employees tend to form cliques both among peers (horizontally) and among managers at different levels of the organization (vertically). These cliques in firms with less than almost total objectivity serve the dual purpose of providing social and personal relationships for those naturally drawn together because of similar interests and perspectives,[5] and as a means of furthering individual self-interest through group relationships.

In Wildcat these cliques are both personal and opportunistic. The more attractive stenographers and secretaries in this company, which is noted for its personable clerical workers, tend to form groups or personal horizontal cliques. The opportunistic cliques are both horizontal and vertical and serve the self-interest of those involved for purposes other than promotability, since this is not a prime consideration.

There is also the vertical clique of Applewhite who wants an interdepartmental transfer, his prospective superior, Hawkins, head of the leasing department, and to a lesser degree Schmidt, who has a semipersonal relationship with Applewhite. Applewhite's participation in this clique will better his chances of transfer, or so he believes. This association offers Hawkins a closer relationship to Schmidt, his supervisor, through Applewhite, and serves Schmidt's purpose of being more closely informed through

Applewhite of the informal and unofficial actions at the lower levels of supervision.

Cliques in Diversified are, as far as can be determined, completely personal or at least designed for mutual benefit in serving company interests. All the management people are convinced that personal relationships will not influence promotability, and cite cases in support of their conclusions. In this company with high corporate objectivity, promotions are based on ability only, and the management employees observe and analyze each advancement.

In one case, two men were being considered for a promotion. One had a very close personal relationship with a higher level manager, but the other man was considered by their peers and supervisors to be more qualified. The more qualified man was promoted. The cliques in Diversified apparently do not serve opportunistic purposes.

The opposite situation exists at Amalgamated where many cliques are opportunistic or predominately opportunistic rather than personal, although it is often difficult to separate the two. These cliques, both vertical and horizontal, encompass not only the people in a given department, but cross interdepartmental lines and even plant facilities and include the headquarters. Most managers above the first two lower levels of supervision informally consider it occupational suicide to lose contact with their cliques regardless of their geographic location or their degree of geographic mobility.

The promotability of the individual in some cases can rather accurately be estimated by his membership in the proper cliques. One of the larger cliques is in the R & D Department at the headquarters location. Many of the promising young executives are sent to the headquarters for technical experience in research and development, knowledge believed important to operating managers for continued product superiority.

This clique is permanent, although the membership constantly changes as managers move in and out of the department. The members have been selected from the various plant facilities as bright young men and most, although not all of them, have in common a degree of opportunism and a great deal of self-interest. The clique absorbs those who are opportunistic, or intuitive enough to recognize its existence and importance, and rejects all others.

The members, almost without exception, live in a certain section of the city which makes social and personal relationships more convenient and almost guarantees membership in the clique. These social and personal relationships carry over into the work situation with the obvious interpersonal relationships of the members.

The degree of promotability is much greater for the members than that for nonmembers, a condition not fully recognized by the nonmembers. The levels of management attained by the members as compared with nonmembers indicates a discernible difference. Ex-members, regardless of present location, on the average move more than one level higher within three years. Of course the ex-members of the headquarters clique were members of other cliques prior to transfer to the headquarters organization and are active members of cliques now. Most of them have maintained the interpersonal relationships with previous members of the clique.

After several years, many ex-members are in a position to nominate the new members by selecting employees for promotion and transfer to R & D, thus providing membership for the permanent clique and continuing the cyclical impetus for promotability.

Cliques in Amalgamated are numerous and often interrelated, with branches of one clique existing for various purposes. Most are informal, though some border on the formal, and they are often directly related to maintenance of the *grapevine* (discussed later). Vertical cliques are assumed to be in the interest of those at the lower level with these managers offering friendship and interest in the same outside activities for the privilege of associating with those at higher levels. Close vertical relationships are fairly common, but not nearly as common as horizontal personal relationships.

Vertical cliques often provide those at the higher level with detailed information on local operations or even on union matters.

The lower ranking individuals *swap* confidences with their supervisors and offer information which provides insights and may alter company decisions. The lower ranking individual is directly exercising control over a situation. Some studies indicate that in these cases the lower ranking individual is being used by higher management to his own detriment,[6] but in Amalgamated all levels seem to benefit.

In all companies studied, with the exception of Diversified, opportunistic cliques existed. (Opportunism was even greater in some companies than in Amalgamated.) Both personal and opportunistic cliques serve a very useful and necessary purpose for some individuals in those companies with less than total objectivity and have the opposite effect on those who do not participate.[7] The objectivity of Diversified precludes opportunistic cliques and is the only company studied in which promotions were based solely on objective criteria.

In industry in general, the ranking executives consider membership in cliques as inevitable. Ninety-two percent of large businesses report that their managers belong to both horizontal and vertical cliques, and eight percent report that their managers belong to horizontal cliques only. One-half of the American businesses reporting admit that both horizontal and vertical cliques are used in their firms for self-advancement as well as for social reasons.

Socionepotism

Nepotism, the hiring of relatives, exists in many organizations, although most have either formal or informal restrictions. Members of any large company are familiar with the subjective, self-oriented, and protective attitudes of the sponsoring relative. Since pure nepotism is generally recognized and understood, we will not dwell on it here.

Socionepotism is group oriented and contributes to the promotability of those accepted in the group.[8] It is directly related to opportunistic cliques since it is the interpersonal relationship of members of the cliques which provides the impetus for the nepotism. As an example, recall that the members of the permanent opportunistic clique at Amalgamated headquarters, after advancing in their own plants, select the members for the headquarters clique and send them to the R and D department. These sponsorships are for the most part self-perpetuating since many of those selected are the same type as their sponsors, i.e., self-centered, bright young men. They fit in with the clique's concept, both occupationally and socially, of the aspiring executive.

The existence of this clique and the resulting socionepotism are not fully recognized by the Amalgamated management team. Those practicing this type of nepotism are probably not cognizant of the full significance of their actions. They tend to view each interaction as an entity rather than as a part of the complex of interpersonal relationships.

Socionepotism exists to some degree in most companies and in mild situations can be considered as the result of the insistence on corporate conformity, as a part of a broader group philosophy.

The socionepotism in Diversified is not as easily recognized as it is in Amalgamated. The aspiring managers of Diversified do keep in touch, though, with key people at the headquarters location, as one upper level executive pointed out:

> Sure, I keep in touch with many of the managers at my level and above [at the headquarters]. I have to coordinate our activities . . . [and] keep in touch with the overall organization. These people should know [me] so [my] name will come up when promotions are considered; and personal friendships or at least knowledge of and respect for [my] contributions to the company are very important. To not keep in touch is in my estimation occupational suicide.

This example in itself does not necessarily indicate socionepotism, but discussions with other upper level managers did indicate that it exists, especially in the headquarters location.

Socionepotism may involve small groups as in the case of an Opportunist who selects employees with opportunistic tendencies. Under these circumstances, promotability is affected by interpersonal relationships and the classification which is being perpetuated.

Even though the most highly promotable managers are often promotable as a direct result of socionepotism, this does not detract from their abilities. The management's objectivity, however, can be questioned.

Adoptive Nepotism

Adoptive nepotism usually involves individuals rather than groups. One manager described a situation in his company involving adoptive nepotism:

> Our quality control officer had been around for years and was highly skilled, an exceptionally capable executive. He had his own ideas about quality controls and his methods were effective. He would re-evaluate with some reluctance as changes in our production facilities occurred, and everything was fine.

> This officer was extremely dedicated and was concerned about any adverse effects his retirement might have on our firm, so some years prior to his retirement he began training a replacement. He trained him so well that after he retired the new officer took over and ran it the same way it was run in the past. The trouble is the new officer is so imbued with his predecessor's theories that he can't adjust to changes in our business. It's as if our previous officer were still here but had become inflexible. The end result is stagnation in the whole department, which has an adverse effect on our whole operation.

This is a fairly common example of self-perpetuation through adoptive nepotism. The employee is usually dedicated to his organization and is concerned that his work may not progress properly in his absence. Usually in such situations it is the individual's operational philosophy which is perpetuated, a philosophy which is often outmoded because of the evolutionary processes in industry.

Adoptive nepotism may also result from personal relationships in which one individual is trying to "ride another's coattails." The tendency to assist one's friends is a natural one. But at Diversified this type of nepotism is controlled through objective programs of employee evaluation. The more objective companies have less socionepotism and adoptive nepotism than those with lower objectivity.

The Grapevine

In all organizations, especially in growth companies offering high potential promotability, the grapevine or informal communication, has a profound effect on the morale and even the operations of the business.[9] Rumors based on fact or fancy run rampant. Employees take pride in "being in on the know." Those who are not "tuned in" to the grapevine may find adjustment to the expectations of the company difficult. At the other extreme, those who place too much faith in the grapevine may suffer agonies while waiting for operational changes which never materialize.*

Those employees who because of their positions normally know about planned changes are constantly besieged with pleas for confidential information, and secrets often leak. These plans may be tentative and subject to modification, but once repeated they are usually accepted as fact.

It is obvious that forewarning may be an advantage to an employee, but the erroneous information flowing through the grapevine may be a disadvantage to the company. Such information often has an adverse effect on morale and sometimes on productivity of employees.

Unfortunately, the grapevine is sometimes responsible for ended careers, and is always potentially dangerous. As an example, recall the statement of the manager who said he could end the career of any of his peers by passing word through the grapevine of any normal difficulties.

---

*Most organizations try to squelch rumors which may have a detrimental effect on morale. During a visit to Diversified, the authors attended a companywide talk by Hopkins, vice president of operations, to the employees. His purpose was to calm the fears that the plant operations were moving to a distant city.

Business recognizes the existence of the grapevine. In the authors' survey of the executive and managerial levels of major U.S. companies, 75 percent of the management teams reported some reliance on the grapevine. Twenty-five percent reported that they never rely on it. On the executive level, 8 percent of the executives said their managers rely on the grapevine *a great deal*, 25 percent said *quite a bit*, and 42 percent said *some, but not much*.

The Prudential Insurance Company of America reports that the reliance on the grapevine is "largely a question of timing. Grapevine information is frequently received in advance of formal announcements. Also the identification of real power figures in the organization is an important responsibility of the grapevine system." An executive of another company says that the grapevine is "mostly unreliable."

The grapevine can be detrimental in some companies for those individuals who are rumored to be soon promoted. Often any indication on the part of the individual that he expects the promotion can easily result in a reversal of plans by his supervisors, since such assumptions are normally considered evidence of the person's less than prudent judgment.

Rumors are based on fact, tentative plans, conjecture, and sometimes on intentional fabrication. Some are harmless, but most are not. Some rumors may start as practical jokes because of a person's disgust with the grapevine system, but as with all rumors, they are potentially dangerous. The rapidity with which they spread and return to the originator is amazing even to those with considerable experience in the organization.

The degree of reliance on the grapevine is related to the company's objectivity. For example, in Diversified the grapevine is of little significance. The higher the company's objectivity, the less reason employees have to use the grapevine as a supplementary information channel.

The Corporate Image

Just as each individual projects his personal image which may or may not closely resemble the actual person, a corporation projects its image. This corporate image consists of what the public thinks the corporation is and is controlled by two factors: (1) the employees and (2) the image created through public relations.

The employee's view of the organization is informally projected through his relationships in the community. These include interpersonal and social relationships through which he expresses his opinions of his organization—opinions which are generally accepted as valid by those with whom he comes in contact. In our society all people are judged and categorized by their neighbors and associates, and these judgments influence the corporate image. The employee's socioeconomic status, political views, ethics, and personal life are informally evaluated and are often related by the observers to his organization. What the employees are, or appear to be, may have a profound effect on the corporate image.

The variations in the type of work done for the organization and the resultant divergence in the socioeconomic status of the employees control the neighborhoods they select and consequently the people with whom they most often are in contact. So-called working class people, the laborers and semiskilled workers, normally live near people with similar occupational skills and similar interests. High ranking management employees normally live near and associate with other managers and professional men whose incomes and perspectives are similar.

The corporate image is influenced by all employees among whom there may be a considerable divergence of opinion as to what the company actually is. Production employees subject to lay off obviously view the company differently than upper management employees who are usually protected from fluctuations in the economy. Their security may be based to a larger degree on their assumed continuing value to the firm than is true of manufacturing employees.

The catalyst for divergent views is the company's formal public relations program which is designed to place the organization in the best possible light in the community. Almost all firms are convinced that a good reputation in the community is a necessary ingredient for a successful business.

The second ranking executive at Diversified had this to say about the importance of public relations:

> In our business we're not directly concerned with the attitudes of this community since we have no direct sales outlets here. You might think as a consequence we're not concerned with our acceptance in this city, but just the opposite is true. We are vitally concerned because we have to be to operate effectively.
>
> Our employees and potential employees are members of this community. To be able to hire the best possible people, we must have the proper reputation in the community, a reputation as a fair employer, certainly, but also as a firm that is interested in the welfare of the community. Due to our size and importance to the economy we are expected to do our part as civic leaders. Consequently our Operations Vice President and myself to a lesser degree are active in civic clubs and activities and assist in city planning when our help is requested. This requires the participation of our wives, too, of course.
>
> It's through these activities that we help build the proper reputation for Diversified. This is very important to our employees since it has a direct influence on what they think of the firm and consequently on employee morale.

The public relations activities at Diversified are conducted by the two highest ranking executives. Those at lower levels are not expected to participate and seldom do. The company does project a good corporate image in the community, but how much of it is due directly to public relations activities is questionable. A principal factor is the overall reputation the company has throughout the United States and the economic reliance of the community on the local major plant facility. Most citizens of the community do not recognize the names of the higher level managers which is probably the result of a lack of interest rather than any reflection on the quality of the public relations. Other prominent businessmen have interpersonal relations with the top managers at Diversified through their joint public relations activities and civic interests.

The chairman of the board at Wildcat, Keeton, is a prominent civic leader and has been for a number of years. He has major investments other than his control of Wildcat, and takes pride not only in his community (all companies investigated are located in different cities), but in his personal contribution to the community. Consequently, public relations are stressed at Wildcat, and all management employees and some production people are urged to participate. Although Wildcat's management people aren't concerned with promotability since it is now a nongrowth company, they are expected to create the proper corporate image (and image for their top executive).

One secretary resigned principally as the result of this expectancy.

> I worked for Wildcat for several years and enjoyed it until my superior kept asking me, insisting really, that I represent them in the petroleum secretaries' club. It wouldn't help the community and I couldn't see that it would be beneficial to the company, although I knew it would at least theoretically help my superior in view of the way Mr. Keeton wants us in everything.

> I didn't have to work, so finally I just gave up and resigned. They offered me a substantial increase to stay, but it wasn't the money. It was the time it takes, so I quit.

Most male management employees at Wildcat are quite active in all civic, municipal, and petroleum activities. These activities provide a method of recognition in the company and doubtlessly influence the amount and frequency of salary adjustments, although this was never formally verified. (Informally, it is generally accepted as true by the management team.)

One of the upper level employees expressed what is the general view of the better informed members of management:

> This public relations situation in my estimation receives too much emphasis. In the first place, the recognition for good corporate citizenship goes principally to one of our executives rather than the

company, although I suppose the company may benefit some too. The point is we don't need this much publicity since it has very little to do with the success of our business.

I used to be fairly active, but I learned one thing in a hurry. The average citizen could care less what we do, it's the members of other firms who are aware of it. They are in effect competing with us for the civic assignments which result in the greatest amount of publicity for the firm. This has evolved now until it is pretty well understood which firm will be assigned to the top position, and it rotates year by year.

The jobs usually go to a certain level of the organization and are assigned by title. One person moves out and his replacement takes over. It usually has little to do with the person individually. Of course, there are a lot of lesser civic assignments that involve more work than recognition that most people try to stay away from. They try to con some people into these who don't know any better.

The self-interest even in civic work is evident in the above statement, although there may be individuals in any community who are interested in furthering the welfare of the community rather than their own.

The community leaders tend to form cliques with ranking members of the larger businesses in the community. These are normally opportunistic cliques, a condition which the members are at least generally aware of. The full significance of the cliques may elude some members. Probably these opportunistic cliques are not recognized as such by the citizens of the community.

City managers are automatically included in the municipal cliques for obvious political reasons, and the demands on their time and their wives' time can become a burden. Members of most prominent organizations, owners of small businesses, and some professional men cultivate the city manager. Some have specific motives and others do so because the city manager is an influential member of the clique, whether he chooses to be or not, and a personal acquaintance with him is an indication of belonging to the proper inner circles.

One of Diversified's executives recounted the following situation which occurred while he and a member of another major company were having dinner with the city manager:

We had finished eating and were talking casually, everyone being polite since all three of us were fairly well acquainted but weren't intimate friends, and all of a sudden [the city manager] burst out laughing, I mean he really got tickled. I asked him what was so funny and he said it just hit him how ridiculous this was. He said I was sitting there politicking him and George, George was politicking the two of us, and he was politicking George and me. Which was exactly right, of course.

And then he said he hadn't had an evening at home with his family all week and we probably hadn't either, so why didn't we all go home and tomorrow we could tell everybody all the points we made with each other. And that's exactly what we did.

The upper management members of Amalgamated take an active part in civic and municipal affairs, perhaps to a greater degree than those of Diversified but to a lesser extent than those of Wildcat. As with Diversified and Wildcat, membership in the proper municipal cliques for upper management is frequently automatic since these people are sought by other clique members.

In all companies researched, the significance of automatic acceptance in the municipal cliques was not totally recognized. It seems obvious from the discussions with ranking executives that adequate public relations often required little more than reasonable interest and social skills. Upper executives, unless they refused to participate, were included in the inner circles. Changes in top management because of transfers or promotions resulted in the immediate acceptance of the new top manager, with automatic assumption of the prestige afforded by that position. For members at lower levels of large companies or members of small companies to gain acceptance in the controlling municipal cliques is difficult and may require skill and planning. Some are highly successful and others fail to gain admission to the clique.

Some companies, of course, employ public relations specialists who as a result of their skills and the prestige of their jobs are included in the clique. Sometimes they exert considerable influence on civic affairs in the interests of their companies.

The images projected by Amalgamated, Diversified, and Wildcat were generally quite good.

Executive Isolation

One of the most pronounced and least understood phenomena in industry is the isolation of top executives. Most upper executives have not been given completely factual information by their employees in so long that as one executive put it, "They wouldn't recognize the truth if they heard it."

These top executives are usually told what their employees think they want to hear. Information is *filtered* or slanted, and although no false information is normally given, the end result is much the same.[10] The top executive is denied the knowledge of real reasons and pertinent information.

These top executives normally progressed from lower levels of management and most were guilty of screening information for their supervisor. That they fail to recognize the degree to which they as the top executive are accorded the same treatment is beyond the powers of comprehension of most of their employees in middle management.

In one major company, a new field representative in the automotive division was instructed during his induction to report market conditions and customer attitudes. He soon observed that customers preferred a competitor's automotive engine additive designed to release sticky valves. The competing product was much lighter and more fluid than his company's. He reasoned that customers were reluctant to put his company's sluggish product in their engines. He reported this with a recommendation for improved customer acceptability.

In due time, his supervisor returned the reports and explained that only good news was sent to higher management because they preferred to not be aware of such market conditions. Reports such as his would be considered a criticism of higher management.

Industry recognizes the importance of giving information to supervisors at the right time, under the proper circumstances, and in the acceptable form, all of which are conditions contributing to executive isolation. Twenty-five percent of the top executives in the major companies say their managers always consider this, and

67 percent say it is usually considered. Only 8 percent consider it only sometimes, and in no companies is it disregarded.

Conclusions

Unofficial actions are required in any company regardless of its objectivity, but the degree of reliance on unofficial action is in inverse proportion to the company's objectivity. In firms with high objectivity, "greasing the skids" prior to official action is much less prevalent than in firms with low objectivity, as is the necessity to read, write, and speak between the lines.

The personal image of individuals in firms with high objectivity more closely resembles the individual when viewed with objective standards than it does in companies with less than almost total objectivity. For example, in companies with high objectivity there are few Noncontroversial Conformists because of objective analysis. This does not diminish the value of this type, however, in those companies with less than almost total objectivity.

The degree of reliance on opportunistic cliques and nepotism is a fairly accurate measurement of a company's objectivity, especially its objectivity related to promotability. In those companies with almost total objectivity, opportunistic cliques did not exist or were ineffective. In companies which depended on opportunistic cliques, the degree of total corporate objectivity was low and could be directly related to the prevalence of the cliques.

The grapevine showed a similar distinction, having little significance in high-objectivity companies and increasing significance in low-objectivity companies. The degree of executive isolation could also be measured in terms of corporate objectivity.

These five factors, unofficial actions, the subjective personal image, opportunistic cliques, socionepotism and adoptive nepotism, and the grapevine, are determinants of corporate objectivity. Since less than almost total corporate objectivity (or the company's interest in its own welfare) is undesirable, it is obvious that reliance on these factors in the operation of the business is very definitely not in the best interests of the company, nor is it in the best interests of the management team and other employees.

Literature Cited

1. Merril, pp. 382-403.

2. Leonard Sayles, *Managerial Behavior* (New York: McGraw-Hill Book Company, 1964), Chapter 5.

3. B. von Haller Gilmer, *Industrial Psychology*, 2nd ed. (New York: McGraw-Hill Book Company, 1966), p. 524.

4. Ray Lewis and Rosemary Stewart, "The Way to the Top," in *Readings in Management*, ed. Ernest Dale (New York: McGraw-Hill Book Company), p. 41.

5. William G. Scott, *Organization Theory* (Homewood, Illinois: Richard D. Irwin, Inc., 1967), pp. 87-88.

6. For example, see Dalton, pp. 59-60.

7. von Haller Gilmer, p. 523.

8. Ibid.

9. Davis, *Human Relations at Work*, p. 226.

10. Charles F. Harding III, "The Social Anthropology of American Industry," in *Management and the Behavioral Sciences,* ed. Maneck S. Wadia (Boston: Allyn and Bacon, Inc., 1968), p. 402.

6 : power struggles

Executives in all types of organizations—business, government, union, and education—frequently engage in power struggles within their respective environments. Often these struggles for dominance are not seen clearly. The power seekers in large-scale bureaucratic organizations have developed subtle manipulative skills that allow them to move behind the scenes to gain power and prestige.

> An organization does not typically move by itself in a direction that will benefit the individual power seeker. He must maneuver and manipulate both to change the direction and character of an organization and to strengthen and enhance his own position.[1]

In large organizations, bureaucracy is one of the vehicles used by warring factions to increase their dominance over others and to insure their protection.

Bureaucracy

The bureaucratic system of many large organizations strongly influences the lives and actions of the individuals within it. The complexities of the bureaucratic organization result in rules and procedures that are rigidly followed with such impartiality that the effect on the employees is often overlooked. Bureaucracy is often characterized by: (1) specialization, with experts in every functional field; (2) a rigid hierarchy, with its resulting lines of authority and responsibility; (3) elaborate rules and procedures; and (4) impersonality.[2]

The functional specialists within the organization tend to develop rules and procedures to control and check on the action

74

of the organization so that it conforms to the ideal plan as developed by these experts. As long as managers follow these impersonal rules and do not *rock the boat,* they have a high degree of job security in this type of organization. Often these rules and procedures are stifling to individual initiative and action and result in forced conformity.

The head of a peripheral staff organization described the functions of his organization as follows:

> We're responsible for determining our quality standards and permissible defect rates. This involves continuing in-depth studies of material and production costs and our analysis of customer reaction to maintenance, attrition, and what we call life-cycle considerations. We use highly technical methods and establish our standards. Some of the operations people are always coming around trying to get us to reconsider something or change the standards. I tell them all we do is set the standards. What is done after that is no concern of ours. I tell them it's not our problem. If they want to change something, go to Collins. Don't bother us with it. We have no control over anything anyway. We just do our jobs.

The line managers at Amalgamated are often frustrated by the standards set by this staff organization, as shown by Forney.

> Sure, they set the standards, but you have to have a degree in statistics or something to read the requirements. You try to figure out what the "Standards" mean and you can go out of your mind, but yet you have to meet them. You have to balance your ratios with your production day-by-day, and the standards change all the time. New sheets and new formulas. We try to get some help, and those guys act like we're a bunch of illiterates. They say it's our problem, not theirs. They say their responsibility ends when they set the standards. Well, it seems to me we're all working for the same company, but sometimes I wonder. They don't care about the end result and don't seem to recognize that they wouldn't be needed to prepare standards if somebody didn't have to use them. It's like they have a line drawn between them and us. I don't know why Collins permits it. Hill didn't do anything either. It's worse at [the company headquarters].

This lack of concern for the end result shown by some peripheral staff organizations in large, bureaucratic organizations is fairly common.

The bureaucratic hierarchy depends on rigid organization, rational efficiency, and clear lines of authority precisely defined and controlled by impersonal rules and regulations. Communications within the hierarchy tend to be strictly one-way with very little communication moving upward.

The roles of managers within such organizations are clearly described and have to be rigidly followed for any degree of job security and promotability. Managerial action is slow and paper work is elaborate because individuals protect themselves by checking proposed actions with several persons at several levels within the organization. The system of checks and the managerial fear result in outdated procedures and resistance to change.[3]

Red tape is not only harassing and frustrating to the individuals who have to work under it, but it also tends to crush the initiative of individuals. It distracts them from their jobs and often causes them to think that they are only cogs in the huge machinery of the organization.

Bureaucracy's aim is toward a high degree of impersonality in the performance of duties and in official relations, as well as in the treatment of personnel. Promotion avenues and policies are supposedly governed by impersonal criteria—merit and seniority— which are part of the official stability required in such organizations. Individuals at all levels of a hierarchy must subordinate their interests and goals to those of the organization so that the complex task of the company can be efficiently performed.

The degree of bureaucracy varies with Wildcat, Amalgamated, and Diversified but is so similar that the following statement by Wildcat's president, Schmidt, describes the situation in all three companies.

See that sitting out there by the door? Something ain't it? Cut her finger on a piece of paper the other day. You never saw so much running around in your life, first aid kits and all, and an accident report in triplicate. You've seen 'em, "How could this accident have been avoided?" Sent it in here to me to sign; said, "All employees was instructed to use extreme caution when filing correspondence since paper edges can inflict serious injuries," or some such. Means don't cut your damn fingers on the paper.

Hell, when me and Jake was back in Ranger, we was drilling and had this roughneck named Ed something or other . . . and he hollers at Jake and says, "Jake it's on my foot!" He says, "Get it off my foot!" And Jake says real calm like, "Move your foot back boy, ain't nothing on your foot." Old Jake was right, there wasn't nothing on his foot, there wasn't, including no toes on his foot. We got us a tourniquet on him and Jake took him in to Doc Weir and peeled off a hundred. Said let him know when it was used up, and got some groceries and took'em out to Ed's Missus and the kids out at their shack. Ed showed up six, eight weeks later, didn't say nothing, just went back to work. I'll tell you something else: we didn't fill out no damn accident report.

The question is not whether a company needs or does not need bureaucracy, but how much is required. Bureaucracy is like any other operational consideration which must be controlled through the corporate operating philosophy or formal programs.

Line Versus Staff

Power struggles are more easily seen in the attitude of those managers engaged in line (direct production) activities toward members of the operational staff and peripheral staff organizations, which is often one of mild derision.[4] This attitude is sometimes coupled with envy for the status and prestige of these staff members, especially if they have the ear of upper executives.[5] The line people think that they are under more pressure (for production which is measurable) and that the managerial skills required for their duties are greater.

At most levels, staff members report to line executives, and their salary adjustments and promotability may be directly or indirectly controlled by the line organization. This is an over simplification, of course, since the staff personnel in bureaucratic organizations exercise much more influence than that with which they are credited. Some staff members may be outranked formally by only the top executive.

The attitude of the line people toward staff members is sometimes reflected in half-serious comments such as, "I wish I had it as easy as you staff jockeys." Many of those making such comments have been or may be staff members in the future. These comments are brought about by the contrast between, as one executive explained, "the line philosophy of 'expediency'. . . [and] the staff philosophy of 'making haste slowly.' "

In many bureaucratic organizations it is recognized that some individuals are only capable of the normally slower pace of the staff. But not often recognized is that some line managers are not suited for staff work simply because they lack the functional literacy required for the volumes of paper work handled on staff assignments. At higher levels of line management, staff employees and secretaries may take care of the literacy requirements for the line manager, though how high a functionally illiterate line manager can rise is, of course, uncertain.

The bureaucratic organizations may require that line managers gain staff experience, usually at the higher levels of the organization and often at the headquarters location—such as at the R & D department in Amalgamated. Most organizations prefer, however, that the bright young men obtain this experience on the operational staff assignments, that is, assignments in the staff organizations which directly support the line operations rather than in peripheral staff functions such as R & D. These organizations consider this experience to be valuable and even mandatory for the well-rounded manager since they think it supplies insights into the bureaucratic operations of the organizations.

What operational staff assignments really provide is a wealth of knowledge about official and unofficial actions, cliques, political maneuvering and socionepotism and adoptive nepotism— information which is invaluable to the aspiring manager in his adjustment to company expectations. Consequently, such assignments are the company's informal training programs for adapting the individual to his corporate environment. The lower the objectivity of the firm, the more valuable this training becomes.

The operational staff organizations normally have more permanent and semipermanent members, especially at the first three lower levels of supervision, than do line organizations. These are the Technicians with limited promotability. (They are more specialized at each higher operational level of the company.) In addition, the higher-ranking staff managers may have less mobility than their line counterparts, adding stability to the staff organizations.

Technicians in the operational staff organizations are the "power behind the throne" since they not only handle the routine operations, but as *experts* they determine policy and operational philosophy. They are limited only by the convictions of the line manager who not only relies on them but can often be influenced by them; or they are limited by higher levels of the line or staff organizations.

One line manager at Amalgamated related an incident which made clear to him just how influential some Technicians can be.

> I recommended a change in our assembly-line procedures which would be of considerable benefit. It was technical and was sent up our organizational hierarchy in the usual manner until it reached [company headquarters] for consideration. It was routed to the head of the proper department and then through progressively lower levels of supervision until it reached the first-level specialist.
>
> He didn't like it and prepared an answer saying why it wouldn't work. It went back up step-by-step until the Executive V.P. signed it and started it back again. Nobody but the specialist knew what it was all about anyway. So I called the specialist to discuss it. He asked who am I to question the Executive V.P. So you have a first-level staff specialist telling a line section head how to run his business.

The line managers above the third level in growth companies may advance at such a rapid rate and their areas of responsibility broaden to such a degree that their limited experience at each level is insufficient to permit comprehensive knowledge of the technicalities of their assignments. They consequently are little, if any, better prepared technically for these assignments than many of their employees. They must under these circumstances rely on the judgments and actions of their supporting staff organizations. The staff people in key positions become quite adept at handling not only routine and technical operational matters, but to a large degree are more than instrumental in forming policy and making management judgments.

The staff members recommend the actions which control the operation of the business and sometimes, for all practical considerations, indirectly run the business. Such staff members in companies with less than almost total objectivity often, through unofficial actions, protect their supervisor from his own lack of technical knowledge and sometimes from his naivety. The staff people consider these subtle *end runs* as necessary for successfully operating the business and for protecting the supervisor who is inexperienced, lacks knowledge, or perhaps is incompetent.

Thus, we find situations such as the one at Amalgamated in which the naive supervisor suggested to a dictatorial manager that he increase production and the results were disastrous. On the other hand, managers of other departments receiving the same suggestion did not insist on *results at any price*. Production in their departments did increase gradually. Thus, the supervisor's naivety was revealed by the Dictator's actions and veiled by the actions of the other types of managers.

In decentralized, democratic organizations, upper management relies heavily on staff members, and decisions are usually made by the influential staff personnel. This is generally true of Amalgamated and to a lesser degree of Diversified. (Recall that the plant manager and the president of Diversified have dictatorial management approaches.) The levels of management and operational staff between the president of Diversified, a subsidiary of a conglomerate, and the plant are, however, more democratic, with an executive committee providing leadership at the subsidiary's home office.

The classification and abilities of the top executive of any organization deeply influence the company's success, and dynamic leadership is required for continued corporate success. It is sometimes overlooked, however, that the supporting staff organizations also exercise a considerable amount of control of the organization. These staff members are predominantly Technicians at the third and lower levels of supervision, even though they may operate at much higher levels of the organization's structure. The first-line supervisors who are ultimately responsible for the company's production are, due to company expectations, also usually Technicians. The Technicians, both line and staff, are very influential on the business operations.

The higher ranking line and staff members who are not Technicians determine the policy or framework within which the business operates, but even here the staff Technicians influence policy decisions.

Defined Versus Actual Authority

In the continuous hassle between power seekers, members of the operational staff organizations are often in a position to exert more real authority than their titles or job descriptions indicate.[6] The degree of control exercised by some of these staff people is seldom recognized by the line managers at lower levels and may not be recognized by line managers at higher levels. Some line managers fail to perceive the extent to which they are influenced directly and how unofficial actions limit their direct control.

The degree of management of managers by their staff or line employees is influenced by the manager's classification. Dictators are more difficult to influence directly; consequently, staff or line employees resort to unofficial actions. Noncontroversial Conformists can be approached more directly. Their managerial approach often encourages direct participation and support from their employees, although employees also resort to unofficial actions.

One Technician quoted earlier commented on responsibilities being given to those people, himself included, who could and would accept them. This willingness of managers regardless of their positions to accept responsibilities, including those not within the limits of formal assignments, provides a means for many of obtaining actual authority far beyond the defined authority.

The balance between actual and defined authority is not a static condition for most individuals because transfers, promotions, and removal of supervisors will affect this relationship. The rapid movement in the upper levels of Amalgamated with the resultant changes in classifications of managers, for example, partly determined the degree of actual authority experienced by the operational staff members, and even determined which of the staff managers would have the greatest authority.

Corporate Self-Perpetuation

The democratic organizations, which rely on group participation, and others to a lesser extent are self-perpetuating in that no one individual is necessary for continuing the corporate operations. All employees are expendable. The organization continues to exist even though key people leave. It seems to run of its own momentum—a momentum which is chiefly provided by the stabilizing influence of the supporting staff organizations.

The expectations of an organization tend to remain substantially the same throughout the years, and the self-perpetuating company tends to perpetuate its own corporate image. Only a formal corporate reappraisal with appropriate formal action can alter this in a brief period. Of course, all large and continuing firms change gradually over an extended period.

Conclusions

Organizational bureaucracy, power plays between executives, defined versus actual authority, and corporate self-perpetuation are all manifestations of the malady infecting less objective companies. This sickness results from the efforts of certain groups to control their environment for either self-protection or increased status and prestige within the organization.

The cure is often bitter medicine. Top management alone, through strong leadership, must be willing to take strong corrective action when managers are engaged in struggles which divert their attention from company goals. Management must work to establish an environment where executives work together as an integrated team and also must establish objective criteria to measure executive contributions toward company goals.

Literature Cited

1. Eugene E. Jennings, *An Anatomy of Leadership (New York: Harper and Brothers, 1960)*, p. 33.

2. Merril, pp. 382-403.

3. Davis, *Human Relations at Work,* p. 447.

4. Perrin Stryker, *A Guide to Modern Management Methods* (New York: McGraw-Hill Book Company, 1954), p. 116.

5. Jay, pp. 147-152.

6. Dill, Hilton, and Reitman, *The New Managers,* p. 13.

7 : what limits promotability?

Basic to promotability is a sound balance between self-interest and company interest. The basic drives of most striving managers result from such psychological concepts as achievement, ego, and power aspirations. If properly motivated by these drives, most managers instinctively develop the necessary social, educational (formal or informal), and communication skills to advance in their companies.

Also basic to promotability and perhaps more important than the preceding requirements is the ability to recognize the formal and informal expectations of the executive organization and the ability and willingness to adapt to these expectations. This involves understanding what activities should be engaged in to perform a job successfully. If the manager and his supervisor agree about where he should apply his efforts for the good of the organization, then his perception is *correct*. If the manager is *incorrect* in his perception, he may expend a great deal of effort without being successful.[1]

Situations like this may occur when a lower-level manager believes that the best way to win promotion is to become highly knowledgeable in his technical specialty, such as chemical engineering. If this proficiency is considered by upper management to be an important qualification for promotion, then his efforts to improve himself may pay off. If, however, broad managerial ability is considered by upper management to be most important, then he has wasted his time and effort.

The mutual understanding between the individual managers and the organization as to just what is expected of them is very important. Organizations devote considerable effort in attempting to motivate employees to exert more effort on their jobs but often give considerably less attention (especially at the upper-management level) to directing such effort.[2] Organizations need to establish clearer understanding of the Expectancy Balance (EB) among the management personnel. The better the understanding between the manager and the organization concerning what is expected, the more rational and objective will be the assessment of the manager's performance.

With an understanding of what the organization expects of him, the individual can make sound decisions in directing his efforts toward the company goals and for his own benefit. Likewise, the organization has a more objective means of making promotions, transfers, or separation decisions regarding the individual manager.

Because promotions are signs of success and significantly influence the aspirations of the management team, they must be used judiciously by top management. Antony Jay makes the following observation.

> I sometimes suspect that the tremendous significance of promotions and appointments is not fully realized in the corporations. You can issue directives and policy statements and messages to staff until the wastepaper baskets burst, but they are nothing compared with promotions. Promotions are the one visible, unmistakable sign of the corporation's standard of values, an irrevocable declaration of the qualities it prizes in its staff, a simultaneous warning and example to everyone who knows the nature of the job and the qualities of its new incumbent. Men who have worked diligently and successfully and then see those who have worked less diligently and less successfully promoted above them start to read the management want ads in the paper the following morning.[3]

The requirements for promotability can be generalized as (1) sufficient self-interest and (2) sufficient perception and adaptability.

Busted Britches

Nonpromotability most often results from the individual's failure to have sufficient self-interest, motivation, sensitivity to the environment in which he works, and failure to adapt as his environment and job assignments change. But situations may arise over which the individual has only limited control.

A previous plant manager now assigned to a staff position explained how he became nonpromotable.

> I used to be plant manager at our Texas facility and had been there about four years. This plant has always been sort of a stepchild due to the necessity for its location. Maintenance expenses on the production facilities and capital retirements have always been much higher than for the other plants, and we still ship production facilities there from other plants in anticipation of this. Of course, this can't be prevented due to the corrosive atmosphere down there which everybody recognizes.
>
> I was doing quite well with production higher than the previous plant managers and had maintenance and retirements down a little. Then we got a new general manager, and he started pushing for maintenance control. I tried to tell him you couldn't improve much and so did some others, what with the saltwater all the hell over everything, but he wouldn't listen.
>
> Finally, I got frustrated and told him I was doing as well or better than anyone else and if he thought he could do better why didn't he run it himself. I was sore.
>
> Well, that did it, I committed the cardinal crime—insubordination. Two weeks later I was here, and I've been here ever since. My career is ended. He just won't tolerate any back talk. I found out the hard way. This happened almost five years ago, and I'm too old to go with another company. That's all there is to it.

Other managers interviewed consider the individual in this example as an above-average manager and were quick to point out that no other managers have produced better results in this particular plant. They also recognize that insubordination is not tolerated ·by their supervisor, who seems to feel completely justified in his evaluation of this manager. The manager's peers consider this situation as an unfortunate personality conflict.

A manager in Amalgamated explained an odd corporate philosophy:

> I used to work for another electronics firm, and they really pushed for production, which was O.K. with me. I can work as hard as the next guy.
>
> My line produced as much as any of the others and more than most. You won't believe this, but upper management expected you to come in on Sundays too, not to work, but just to be seen on the premises—supposed to show how much you loved the damn place.
>
> Well, I have a family. What are you supposed to do, live at the plant? Lots of the foremen came down to the lounge on Sunday and drank coffee for a couple of hours. I did a few times, and then said to hell with it—it's not worth it. It would make more sense if you worked at something. But just being seen, why it's ridiculous.
>
> I started to get passed over on promotions, and I finally asked why. My boss said they weren't sure about my attitude and for me to think about it. Attitude! How does that grab you? So I quit and came here.

Such unreasonable expectations are quite common and are not restricted to one company. Failure to adapt to them can and often does affect promotability.

Another manager's company interest created for him an undesirable image:

> All right, so maybe I'm stupid. But I've been taught all my life if something is worth doing, it is worth doing well—and that's my problem.
>
> We have some of the most outdated procedures you can imagine, and periodically we get instructions which just make things worse. I don't think it's right to just sit back and take it. What kind of men are we anyway? So I buck the system, try to point out the improvements we can and should make.
>
> You know what that makes me? A troublemaker. I have the reputation up the line for being a troublemaker. But the other supervisors all agree

we aren't operating properly, so it's not just me. They always want me to take exception to things and try to get things corrected. They must figure I'm dead anyway, and they're right. I'm not going any place with this company.

This supervisor's unwillingness to conform to his company's expectations of nonobjectivity has obviously influenced his promotability.

One manager's high degree of promotability ultimately led to his dismissal.

I worked for an electronics company and was considered one of the brighter young executives with the result that I moved up rather rapidly. I would get just enough experience to almost know what I was doing and then get promoted and be in over my head again. It worried me, not knowing my jobs technically as well as I should, but I justified it on the basis of being a manager working through people.

Then we had a crackdown in the whole company, and I just couldn't produce. I simply didn't know enough. I had to resign before they fired me. They don't like to bust middle-management people since they usually become unsatisfied employees, so I had to get out. I feel like I was the victim of circumstances since I couldn't very well turn down promotions. I like it better here now that I've adjusted. I don't make as much, but I have more confidence in myself. And I'm moving ahead again.

The causes of demotions, dismissals, and nonpromotability are myriad and include such considerations as personal problems, personality conflicts, unwillingness to produce, inadequate preparation for the assignment, basic incompetency, dishonesty, and others. When the individual is capable but nonpromotable, he is usually unwilling or unable to adjust to company expectations.

Dead-End Jobs

In many organizations certain jobs are maintained for those managers who for any reason are no longer capable of performing at their level. These sinecures are usually staff assignments, but may not be. Some organizations recognize that a certain amount of executive attrition will occur, and the positions are held for these relatively incompetent, but usually deserving, managers.

These positions are often at the upper level of the organization, making it possible to *promote* individuals out of the main stream of the operations. The jobs may require certain skills which those being *dead-ended* possess.

Other jobs are created to meet these needs, usually with the title of *Assistant to*. These jobs normally are eliminated as soon as the persons filling them retire or leave the organization. This often results in disappointment for those managers who had hoped to be promoted to fill one of these created positions and discover that the job title has been discontinued.

These two types of sinecures are maintained for two reasons: corporate benevolence and *skeletons in the closet*.

Many corporations feel an obligation to take care of those employees who have been valuable and loyal for many years but who have become incompetent, or partially incompetent, because of advanced age, illness, or inability to adjust to changing conditions.

One top executive gave this explanation of corporate benevolence:

> We here at Amalgamated feel an obligation to our people. Those who have been with us for years are usually loyal, hard-working employees. Unfortunately, some become less able to cope with the demands of the business eventually, and we have to have a method of taking care of them without impairing the functioning of our business. We have several permanent jobs we save for these people and create others as necessary. We are quite reluctant to create unnecessary jobs and seldom do this, but we do place these people in jobs that make it possible for them to participate within the limits of their abilities. This gives them a sense of accomplishment, and we do get the benefit of their abilities.

> We don't talk about this sort of thing for obvious reasons. These people prefer to believe they were selected for the jobs due to their experience and special qualifications, and we prefer to keep it that way.

I think any business should have this much consideration for its employees. We must recognize, too, that the day may come when any one of us may have to fill such a position. If I ever do, I know I'll want to be made to feel just as valuable to this company as I ever did. It's not all benevolence, you see.

The skeleton-in-the-closet effect is more difficult to pinpoint. This is one area that most executives were reluctant to discuss.

In some companies those few upper executives who had violated company doctrine—rather than being released—were placed in high-ranking executive positions. Some of these positions were obviously created.

Fear of damaging public relations and personnel relations seems to be the main reason for not dismissing top executives. Dismissals could easily be considered as a reflection on the judgment of the executive's supervisors. As a result, they are reluctant to openly admit errors in selecting top managers. Of course, they may not have made an error in judgment. Any individual can for a number of reasons react to pressures in ways unsuited to the corporate environment.

A middle manager discusses such a situation in his company.

I doubt you'll find anyone around here who will admit to what really happened; and, of course, I don't know for sure, but it's really pretty obvious and is common knowledge. A top executive was taking some kickbacks on purchases. This has been substantiated. And apparently he got caught because he was suddenly moved to a staff position. A lot of the people thought it was a promotion, but some of them know better. They're afraid to admit what happened, so they keep quiet about it. He won't get any further, but he's lucky at that. If I'd done it, I'd have been fired right then.

Manpower Analyses

Periodically most companies conduct personnel appraisals to evaluate their employees for promotability. Some major firms have no formal approach, though, and prefer to judge their people on a *day-to-day* basis.

The degree of objectivity in analyzing employees is generally related to the corporate objectivity. Those organizations with formal programs use a variety of methods—all designed to give insights into the qualifications of the employees. Although some appraisal methods may be superior to others, it is not the method's which indicate the degree of objectivity. Actually, objectivity may depend on the philosophy of top management.[4]

Many companies employ a joint or committee technique in employee appraisal. This approach is sound in theory. Supposedly, it forces the manager to justify his opinion of the selected employee and serves to temper opinions that may be extreme, either favorably or critically. For upper-level positions, appraisal by more than one person is essential. At the same time, the realistic approach accepts managerial ratings of lower-level personnel where such factors as advancement-potential and the like are of less consequence.

Use of the committee appraisal technique may result in false objectivity. If the other managers are unacquainted with the employee's work, their natural inclination would be to approve the opinions of the supervisor. It would be a committee appraisal in name only.

If the committee approach is to be used with any success, the appraisal should be made by persons who are (1) in a position above that of the employee being appraised, (2) acquainted with his responsibilities and performance, and (3) objective throughout the process. (Even then, objectivity may fall by the wayside.)

One manager from Amalgamated commented on his company's joint appraisal meetings.

> If it weren't so serious, it would be funny. These meetings are usually a farce. Everybody has some people they want to push ahead, but some feel more strongly about it than others. But remember, those doing the analyzing have one primary motive—self-protection—and this is where they can practice it openly.
>
> Here's how it works. If your production is up, maintenance down, etc., you are in a position to push your men for promotion. If you want a reputation for developing people, now is the time to push them. So

under these circumstances, the managers can do no wrong. They are capable, and those at least reasonably qualified are recommended for advancement.

But if production is down, the shoe's on the other foot. Here is where you get self-protective. Maybe six months ago your people were capable and deserving of promotion, but now suddenly they aren't. It isn't your fault production is down. Obviously, it's theirs. "I'm concerned about Benny," you say. "He has been doing quite well, but lately he has been letting things slip a little." See, it's his fault, not yours. Then you go on about how you've been trying to develop Benny. And listen to everybody else whose production is down show concern for their Bennys.

The funny thing is this is all done with a straight face, very seriously, and it's all recorded as gospel. You have to play ball with the others in the meeting, too. You try to get objective about something, and they'll get a piece of you right there—self-protection again. They do it with righteous indignation. Man, those meetings can chew you up if you aren't careful.

And then some guys want to push their men harder than others do. Sometimes this is just loyalty to the men, and in others it's a way to get a reputation for developing people, or at least of standing up for your men. So you get an unequal measurement of abilities. Like, for example, you have this meathead, and everybody knows he is, but his boss is pushing him. So everybody ignores his shortcomings and makes favorable comments, like, "Benny sure is good to his mother," or some such garbage.

What do I do? If you're going to play ball, you have to play it in the same ball park. I play ball—that's what I do. You can't knock heads with the system. Nobody is really fooling anybody much anyway. Hell, isn't it?

All companies with less than almost total corporate objectivity conduct meetings with varying degrees of objectivity of appraisals, with some companies more objective than others. However, one can readily question whether those promoted in companies with less than almost total objectivity are the best qualified if the personnel-analyses meetings are used as the criteria for judgment.

Running Scared

One of the most appalling conditions in many organizations is caused by the fear that many managers have, especially those in the middle management or higher levels of the organization. Those individuals who are dependent on their organizations for a livelihood as a result of many years with the company or those who for any reason do not wish to leave the organization are captives of their company. Thus, the company exercises control over the individual. He must adapt to what the company expects of him if he is to remain promotable or perhaps even to retain his position.

Fear of authority, of a superior, of changing job requirements, or of job responsibilities, or failure[5] torments many managers. Fear of nonpromotability, or even fear of being promoted to an undesirable job or to an undesirable geographic location torments others.

Fear, reduced to its most basic form, is fear of the control the company exercises over one's destiny. Few managers are fortunate enough to escape this anxiety.

One manager was shocked at the amount of fear which permeated the headquarters organization of his company.

> Everybody up there was running scared. I never saw anything like it. They spend days writing one paragraph, getting it just right, before they send a recommendation or a letter or anything up to the top executives. They figure and plan and analyze everything before they do anything, and then they stand there and shake.
>
> I could smell fear when I walked in. That's all it is, just plain fear. . . . I don't know how we stay in business, I swear I don't, not with that kind of an operation. They send you up there for an education on product knowledge. You get an education all right—on how to run scared.

A manager in another company recognized his own fear at a low level of the organization.

> I have ulcers. You know what causes ulcers? Fear. Plain unadulterated fear. I'm so damn shook up all the time it's no wonder. I fight this job

day in and day out, and nothing seems to get any better. I'm going to get thrown out on the street one of these days. You know what? Most of the managers on jobs like this are terrified.

I'm sick and damn tired of being scared. But what can you do? Either take it or get out. I'm looking for a way out.

Fear is not restricted to the middle and lower levels of management. A recent study disclosed that added responsibilities increased pulse rates appreciably. Experienced executives, when required to make high-level talks or presentations, almost without exception had increased pulse rates, many well above 130 heartbeats a minute.

One middle manager explained how he had recognized his fear and tried to control it.

The pressure was starting to get to me, so I talked with my family doctor about it. He gave me some pills to help prevent ulcers. My stomach was cutting up on me. But I wanted to get to the root of the problem, so I made an appointment with a psychiatrist. Paid him $25 to listen to him cuss out industry in general. He impressed on me it was fear. I guess I knew it all the time but didn't want to admit it. So now I get up every morning and say, "To hell with the world, I'll do the best I can." It helps. Not a total solution, but it helps. What you have to do is recognize that most of the others are scared too.

Ulcers and similar symptoms of corporate fear are vocationally acceptable since causative factors are seldom considered in proper perspective. Evidence of fear is not acceptable, however.

The first time you show a sign of weakness, the wolf pack is on you. They may not mean to, but the result is the same. All it takes is to let someone know you have troubles, and the talk starts. That's all it takes to end your career. You have to pretend that all is right with the world, even if you're ready to jump out a window. Of course, I don't have any problems myself [laughter].

It is a reflection on industry in general, and perhaps on our society, that the demands on many managers produce such unfortunate results. Increased corporate objectivity and concern for production through motivated people can alleviate this situation.

The Fallacy of Growth and Promotability

Rapid growth of a company increases the opportunity for promotability since additional positions are created in a growing company. Many managers erroneously assume that the increase in available positions automatically offers greater opportunity, but, in fact, it often lessens the promotability of many managers.

Growing companies must consider not only the necessity of filling current vacancies, but must also consider the high-level positions which will become available. Consequently, many such companies groom young managers, including college recruits, for these positions.

One manager explains how he found out about the fallacy of growth and promotability.

> When we began to grow rapidly, I automatically assumed my chances for promotion would be greatly increased. They weren't. The company figures you have to move the men so fast to get them to the upper levels of management that those of us who are experienced are expected to run the business while we train the kids to be our bosses. I'm 38 and have 27 years to go with the company, but suddenly I'm too old. One of my friends is too old at 31 to progress in his department. The age limit is 28.
>
> I'm interested in the company . . . but I'd be better off personally if we didn't have so many openings. When things are tougher economically, they have to promote the capable people, the ones who can produce now. It may sound ridiculous, but a mild recession with retarded growth would make me promotable again. I can't believe the whole situation is completely rational.

It is questionable whether the company policies which include arbitrary rules for promotability are in the best interests of either the company or the individuals. Companies having arbitrary age limits at the various levels of the organization usually modify these to accommodate internal or external operational considerations. Consequently, the age limits tend to be raised during nongrowth periods and be lowered during periods of rapid expansion.

One manager in a growth company made this observation:

> We have to hire 20- or 21-year-old kids, preferably college graduates, in order to meet our age requirements for promotion. They have to reach our third level by the time they are 28 or they are through.

> Some are quite immature, so we play nursemaid for several years or more. I mean we literally raise these kids. A few are mature, some even balding, and act much older. Sometimes I wonder if these really mature youngsters will be senile before they retire. Maybe we are cutting the yardstick off on one end to make it longer on the other. I'm too old at 34 to reach our fourth level.

Industry can ill afford the results of using nonobjective criteria—such as arbitrary age limits, personality conflicts, personal images, and conformity to unreasonable expectations—when deciding which employees are nonpromotable. An objective criterion for nonpromotability is a lack of ability.

Literature Cited

1. Porter and Lawler, p. 24.

2. Ibid., p. 175.

3. Jay, p. 178.

4. Bowman, pp. 6 ff.

5. Abraham Zaleznik, "The Human Dilemmas of Leadership," in *Management and the Behavioral Sciences*, ed. Maneck S. Wadia (Boston: Allyn and Bacon, Inc., 1968), pp. 202-204.

8 : the technician

The Technician—the loyal, hard-working, company-oriented manager whose personal creed parallels the Protestant Ethic is the backbone of every organization. Normally, he lacks the perception to correctly identify his company's expectations and therefore misdirects his talents. His promotability is uncertain.

Interview with A Technician

Interviewer: How do you approach your job?

Technician: I take my work seriously, and I do the best I can to see that the job is done properly.

Interviewer: You feel rather strongly about doing the job properly, don't you?

Technician: Yes, I do. This is a staff assignment, as you know, and it's our responsibility to operate in such a manner that we support the line operation. I think we have a very urgent responsibility. The line couldn't operate effectively if we didn't provide the support they need.

Interviewer: Do all the staff people feel like you do?

Technician: Unfortunately, they don't. Most do, I suppose, but some don't. You'll find in any staff organization in this company . . . those who do very little.

Interviewer: Why is that?

Technician: Some just don't care. They think if they do what they are generally responsible for that's enough. They don't always consider the end result. They float. You have to consider that some of these staff people didn't make it for one reason or another on the line, so they have lost interest to some degree. Some think they weren't treated fairly. Perhaps some weren't. But there are others who show a real interest.

Interviewer: Why didn't some make it on the line?

Technician: Various reasons. Some are not aggressive enough. Some may have been in the wrong place at the wrong time. Some of them prefer staff work.

Interviewer: Why?

Technician: It's less demanding on your time if you want it to be, and you aren't so easily measured. I don't view it that way, though. I think if you have the proper attitude it's no different than line jobs.

Interviewer: You work at it like a line job?

Technician: I do. I've been on the line, and I work just as hard here. But not everybody does. Some of the line managers could work at it harder too in my estimation.

Interviewer: They don't all dig in?

Technician: No, they don't. It depends on where they are and at what level. The first-line men in most jobs don't have much choice. A few jobs offer a way to float some. But the higher you go, the more chance there is to pay less than 100 percent attention to the job. Some work at it hard, some don't.

Interviewer: How do you feel about those who don't?

Technician: If I were running it, which I'm not, I'd make some changes quick.

Interviewer: Fire a few?

Technician: No, I don't think that would be necessary. I'd just see to it that they worked more for the company. You can call golf public relations if you want to, but I'd make sure it was.

Interviewer: Some do that?

Technician: Sure. Golf or anything else. Of course that's at the higher levels. I'd see they didn't waste company money on unnecessary expense too.

Interviewer: Oh?

Technician: It's hard to tell what's justified and what's not, I know that, but I'd take a real close look at expense vouchers. A trailer hitch on a company car looks a little suspicious to me when it's being driven by a fisherman or hunter.

Interviewer: They do that?

Technician: I don't know. You hear things.

Interviewer: You wouldn't do that yourself if others do?

Technician: I wouldn't. Some of my co-workers might. I don't think it's right.

Interviewer: You feel you owe your company more loyalty than that?

Technician: Definitely. The way I feel about it the company has been good to me, so I'll be good to it.

Interviewer: How specifically has the company been good to you?

Technician: Well, they, I don't know, they appreciate me, my work, I guess. And I have a good job, better than most. And I get my raises right on schedule.

Interviewer: Do you think you'll get another promotion soon?

Technician: It's better to wait and see on those things. You can't bid on them you know.

Interviewer: But it's possible that you will, isn't it?

Technician: I don't know. I thought I had a good chance on [a job] but I didn't get it.

Interviewer: Why?

Technician: I don't really know. This other guy was qualified and he got it. So I'm not kicking.

Interviewer: You wanted it, though?

Technician: Well, sure, I'd like to have it. I'll have another chance, probably.

Interviewer: Probably?

Technician: You can't tell about these things. I really thought I would get the other one.

Interviewer: Do you have any idea why you didn't?

Technician: No, not really. I thought I would. I feel like I was qualified and that I'd earned it, so it upset me a little at first. I worried about it for a while. Sometimes I just can't figure why things happen like they do. I don't see why [a line manager] got promoted to department head for that matter. He never did seem to be too company minded, and yet they promoted him.

Interviewer: Any ideas why?

Technician: No. I just can't see it. They've done it before, too. [cited examples]

Interviewer: Do you mean they don't reward loyalty with promotions?

Technician: Well, I wouldn't say that. I don't know. Sometimes they do. I think maybe some guys fool them into thinking they are loyal and hard working. Maybe that's it.

Interviewer: What do you think it takes to get ahead?

Technician: I always felt if you worked hard, learned your job, and were proficient that you would get ahead.

Interviewer: Does it work that way?

Technician: Well, yes, sure. I have.

Interviewer: But you didn't get that last promotion. And you just said some who weren't necessarily loyal and proficient do get ahead.

Technician: Well, I don't know. Maybe some do, but it just stands to reason that if you are technically proficient and company minded you'll be able to contribute more to the company.

Interviewer: But does that mean you'll get ahead?

Technician: I'd say so. You'd pretty well have to.

Interviewer: Do you think you, or those who are company minded like you are, will rise to the upper levels of management?

Technician: I can't speak for myself but some do. You take [name] and [name], they are company minded and look where they are.

Interviewer: Yes. You feel then that loyalty and hard work pay off in the long run?

Technician: Yes, I do.

Interviewer: Do you think your firm is objective?

Technician: How's that?

Interviewer: Is the company interested in its own welfare?

Technician: Of course. I don't see how it could be otherwise.

Interviewer: They always do everything based on what's in the best interest of the company?

Technician: Yes, I think we all work for the company pretty well.

Interviewer: How about the trailer hitches, golf games, and expense accounts?

Technician: Oh, I see what you mean. Well, those are just a few individuals. Or at least as far as I know they are. I'd straighten that out if I could.

Interviewer: Do you always take a direct approach to your duties, or do you sometimes have to ease into things?

Technician: I just do what has to be done.

Interviewer: You don't prepare people in advance for one of your recommendations, for example?

Technician: No, not much. What's right is right. I don't see the need for it. I just do my job the best way I know how.

Interviewer: Do you pretty well follow the established rules and procedures?

Technician: Almost always. That's what they're for. I don't feel I'm qualified to question the methods we've established. Oh, once in a while I question something, but I follow the instructions until we get it changed. We can recommend improvements, you know. I do quite often.

Interviewer: What do you expect personally from your company?

Technician: Well, I want to be appreciated for my work, and I enjoy being a part of the company. My pay, of course. And a chance to get ahead.

Interviewer: What does it take to get ahead?

Technician: You need to know your job and prepare yourself for the next higher one.

Interviewer: Is that how [some] get ahead?

Technician: Wait a minute. Are you saying that you shouldn't be proficient and all that?

Interviewer: I just wondered if they were. Is that how they got ahead?

Technician: I don't think it is, but that doesn't make it right, does it? A person should get ahead on what he is capable of doing for the company. I don't know why they got promoted. I'll never understand it.

Interviewer: This bothers you?

Technician: Well, some lately, since I got passed over. It doesn't seem right to me.

Interviewer: What qualities do you think are required for promotability?

Technician: Well, I guess the truth is I don't know. There doesn't seem to be a pattern I can follow. I admit I don't understand it.

Interviewer: What do you plan to do in the future to insure your own advancement?

Technician: I'm taking several college courses now, working on my master's, and that should help. And I've been working on a [technical correspondence course] which I don't have to do and things like that.

Interviewer: You feel this will help you get ahead?

Technician: Yes, I think so. I think I'll be advanced before too long.

This Technician was chosen for the interview because of his recognized capabilities and his naiveté which is typical of the Technician, whether he is highly skilled or has inferior abilities.

This Technician was loyal and hard working, although many of his fellow Technicians didn't share these attributes. He felt very strongly about loyalty to his company and repeatedly stressed his desire to instill loyalty in other employees "if he could."

As with most Technicians, he did not recognize the requirements for promotability in his company and was unable or unwilling to adjust to company expectations.

His supervisor was aware of the effect that this naivete and lack of adaptability had on the Technician's promotability:

> Bill is a hard worker and he is highly intelligent, but he gets too wrapped up in his work. I've tried to develop his capabilities, but it's like talking to a stone wall. He is convinced his approach is right, and I don't disagree with that. We'd be better off if every employee were as dedicated as he is. The problem is not everyone is interested in that much dedication.

> Bill is the type who is so concerned with the problem at hand that he can walk right by without seeing you. He is a fine person and is pretty well liked. But he lacks warmth, I guess you'd call it. He's more interested in things than people, and this hurts him. But he can't see it.

> He has been passed over several times, and I doubt he'll ever progress beyond [third-level staff]. We have to have more versatile people. There are others like Bill who are valuable employees but who will never progress very far. I think he may be happier where he is, anyway.

Most Technicians are probably more content being Technicians. They find it very difficult to accept the actual circumstances and prefer to adhere to what they believe is correct. This Technician was unwilling to accept the truth about his promotability. He *reasoned* out his problem during the interview but immediately returned to his conviction that hard work and loyalty would result in promotability—that it would "pretty well have to."

The Technician was also unwilling to recognize his company's nonobjectivity and attempted to justify it. This was probably done for his own benefit rather than for the interviewer's since some Technicians want to believe in the integrity of their companies.

He also used a direct approach and would not recognize the existence of unofficial actions which are often necessary to accomplish a purpose in any company.

Technicians at Diversified

The Technicians at Diversified were convinced that promotability was based on the manager's ability to perform the duties of the next level position. Middle and upper management were well aware that consideration was also given to total potential and that both factors were prerequisites to promotions. Stone, a foreman, confidently explained what promotability was based on at Diversified.

> Promotions are based on the person's ability to do the job he is getting promoted to. It's all based on ability, and friendships don't enter into it. We had a situation here recently where one [man] was a very close friend of his boss, and he was very well qualified for the promotion. But another one got it who was considered even more qualified. So friendships don't influence it. It's based entirely on your ability to do the next level job.

Stone did not recognize the other factor in promotability. A higher-level manager gave a more accurate explanation of promotability at Diversified.

> Promotions are based on the ability to do the next level job. The person has to be totally qualified to handle it. Also we consider the total potential of the individual. So it is a combination of the two. We certainly wouldn't promote anybody on potential alone. They have to be able to do the job first. The requirements get broader at each higher level, too. We have to consider a person's poise and polish above the second level. The higher you go, the more the work becomes administrative, which means working through people. So we consider both . . . ability and potential.

The somewhat naive assumptions of the first-level managers at Diversified about the requirements for promotability are representative of Technicians in other companies also.

Technicians at Wildcat

The Technicians at Wildcat were at the lower levels with the exception of Tate, head of the geological department. Individuals, of course, sometimes change classifications, and it is probable that earlier in his career Tate would have been classified differently. In another company one executive at a high level was reportedly an Opportunist, but when he became unpromotable he reverted to a Technician.

Schmidt had little respect for Technicians but felt that they had a place in the organization:

> We have some of these worker types here, and that's what they're paid for—work. They ain't going nowhere. All they're fit for is manual labor of one kind or another. We always had them and always will. Hell, we had them back when me and Jake was drilling. Had to pay some of them $20 a day and feed them to boot on the rigs. They never made more'n $2 a day in their lives, so they thought they was rich. Didn't have enough push to go out and do anything. Couldn't drill no wells without them, though. Couldn't run no business without them neither.

Technicians at Amalgamated

In Amalgamated the Technicians who would remain as such were either on staff assignments or would in all probability end up on them. A few were on first-level line assignments and had very limited promotability. Most of the line Technicians were classified as Technicians as a result of the company's expectations. At higher levels, they became one of the other classifications of promotables.

Ayers discussed the Technicians at Amalgamated and recognized the problems they faced:

> We have a number of management people who won't progress in our business since they don't understand that job knowledge alone is insufficient. They lack certain qualities. One of these is ambition. They don't want to make the sacrifices that are required, such as mobility for them and their families. Or they don't develop the necessary qualities. Some very capable men never get into the management ranks because they are unable to address a group of men in an informal meeting which foremen must do. You'd be surprised how this can terrify a big burly man who wouldn't be afraid of anything else in this world.

Then some lack the proper grooming and won't or can't learn. And speech is a problem. It's a shame the number of otherwise qualified people we have who use incorrect grammar. This is really a major problem. Our attempts at correcting this have been most unsuccessful. This is probably the most difficult of all problems for someone to overcome. Yet we have to consider it. People are judged on their grammar, and it's something they can't hide. It's a pity, really. College English courses are ineffective—a total loss. I don't have a solution for this—wish I did.

The major problem is the total inability of so many people to recognize that they must learn to find their way through the personal relationships of the organization. They simply are not people oriented. They don't understand, and it's difficult to explain because it's so complicated. I don't know how to teach someone something I find very difficult to define myself. And yet this is the major problem for so many otherwise promising employees.

Ayers is a skilled executive who understands the problems of his capable Technicians and would like to help them. But he realizes that explaining specifically how to adapt to the informal expectations of any organization is difficult since these expectations are usually in a constant state of change. What is required under a manager like Ayers is markedly different than expectations under an Opportunist like Templo.

Although the personal managerial-imposed expectations may change, the requirements of unofficial actions and personal relations usually remain fairly constant. The Technicians normally don't recognize these expectations which are less discernible than specific managerial philosophies.

One company, not a case-study company, evaluates managerial potential in a formalized program which includes a test of the potential manager's ability to use unofficial actions in a group testing situation to accomplish his assigned purpose. This is also a method of teaching aspiring managers the necessity for unofficial actions. It seems most doubtful that this testing technique is considered in its proper perspective. Efforts to obtain a higher degree of corporate objectivity with less reliance on unofficial actions would be more beneficial to the company.

The Technicians at Amalgamated are in a less desirable position than those in some other companies since promotability is based principally on total potential rather than on the ability to do the job. This limits their promotability more than otherwise would be true.

Summary

The Technician classification poses a special problem in that individuals who are highly qualified in most respects lack the perception to recognize the factors which are preventing their promotability.[1] The Dictator interviewed in Chapter 8 stated that it took him 20 years to learn that technical job knowledge was not enough to insure promotability. He did not indicate what stimulated his sudden understanding, but it is probable that an emotional trauma may have resulted from his failure to get a promotion.

Most of those managers interviewed who had been Technicians and had changed their perspective did so as the result of a traumatic experience—sudden recognition of their nonpromotability as a Technician.

The following statement was made by a manager who was suffering from such an experience. He is a young man with some years experience in industry. He has an engineering degree and had progressed satisfactorily with his first employer.

I was selected by this electronics firm for a project manager's job that required specialized training and experience. I talked it over with them in quite some detail before I decided to quit my job and accept their offer.

I moved my family and assumed my new duties. My primary responsibility was the development of a new physical plant. Immediately I began to run into problems. With a job of this magnitude, I anticipated I would be given a number of assistants and would receive the cooperation of various departments. I was lucky to get a secretary, and I just couldn't get the technical help I needed. I didn't know what to do. I was on my own, and I couldn't get anything I needed. I tried to point out that my assignment was totally impossible unless I was supported, but the harder I tried the less cooperation I got.

I couldn't understand it. It doesn't make sense to undertake an important assignment which has a tremendous effect on the company without the cooperation of the whole organization.

So I guess I panicked. I tried to tell the boss and the department heads my problems. I tried to insist on cooperation. I spoke my mind and told the truth in an effort to get some help. . . .

Then gradually I began to get some idea of what was going on. There must have been some rivalry between some top executives and maybe some department heads. I should have found out what was going on before I jumped into it. I guess I took everything at face value at first, and in my efforts to get something done I alienated a lot of people. A straightforward approach just wouldn't work, but that's all I knew how to do.

So I busted it. I had to resign before I got fired. I'd left a good job, and now I was out on the street. I've had some time to think it over now, and I'll never make that mistake again. I still don't know exactly what happened. I know it certainly wasn't all my fault, but I did make some major mistakes.

I shouldn't have attempted to do what I did. And I went about it wrong. I should have sensed there were some frictions and acted accordingly. I should have made some friends first and found a way to get the information I needed afterwards. I guess I did everything wrong.

It makes you doubt your own abilities. I can see now I didn't approach my other job properly, although I got along O.K. there. My formal training is technical, and I just wasn't prepared for a job that required insights into the way the company really works. I'm trained to think in terms of facts and figures and formulas. Many of my friends who are technically trained are having or are going to have the same problem I did. I can see that now. We're just not prepared for this sort of thing.

I've learned my lesson, and I'll never get into a mess like that again. I'm about able to face things now, but you'll never know what this has done to me. I've started over and we'll get on O.K., but I'll never get over this completely. This was a big chance for me and I blew it. Boy, I mean I blew it.

With no knowledge of the situation, this manager attempted to force cooperation from factions with conflicting loyalties. His factual approach was resisted to the point that execution of his assignment became impossible. He attempted a Technician's approach at a high level of the organization, and the results were disastrous.

The Technician's lack of adaptability is a major consideration in industry. Many managers believe that Technicians should remain Technicians since available high-level positions are limited in most companies. This is not a valid argument. Any employee can become more effective if he at least understands the company expectations. Educating Technicians to these expectations, however, is very difficult since they resist viewing their companies objectively.

The truly dedicated Technician who can recognize and accept his situation often makes an excellent adjustment to his organization. His approach is based on hard work and loyalty which can provide a great deal of satisfaction. If he has limited ambition, he well may be a "reasonable adventurer" as defined by Roy Heath in his Princeton study.[2]

Literature Cited

1. Powell, p. 60.

2. Roy Heath, *The Reasonable Adventurer* (Pittsburg: University of Pittsburg Press, 1964).

9 : the dictator

The Dictator—the hard-driving, no-nonsense manager—is a particular breed of executive found throughout industry. Success-oriented, often haunted by a fear of failure, he pushes his people toward perfection for his own benefit and perhaps for that of his company.

An Interview With a Dictator

Interviewer: What is your operational philosophy?

Dictator: Well—if I understand what you mean—how I approach my management team generally?

Interviewer: Yes, what is the managerial approach you use to direct your people?

Dictator: I establish objectives within which the management team operates. We have various goals and budgets. We figure our cost objectives and these are inviolable. We stay within our objectives. We work toward meeting our production goals.

Interviewer: You manage by objectives?

Dictator: Well yes, sure. We have our goals—our budgets, including costs—and I expect all levels of supervision to meet the objectives, stay within the budgets. I don't know any other way you can run a business efficiently.

Let me make this clear. We always plan in advance—without exception. Then we modify our plans for unanticipated situations. We received a large order recently which we didn't anticipate, so we reevaluated our production plans, found out how to do it with the proper priority, and modified our formal plans and objectives accordingly.

110

We have to take the unanticipated into consideration. I'd say we operate about 85 percent scheduled with a 15 percent variable to take care of emergencies. We set up internal goals, goals within the plant operation, and run in a plus-three position. We have to have a cushion.

Interviewer: How do you motivate your people?

Dictator: We follow up. Make sure things are running properly. I hold a production meeting every morning with all people reporting directly to me and the next lower level of production managers. All items we discuss are formally scheduled. If we are doing well on an item, we may reduce the frequency of discussion to once a week. If we have problems, we may schedule it for discussion every day.

Interviewer: Do you use specific techniques such as Critical Path Scheduling?

Dictator: Well, yes and no. We do, but not formally. Going back to the daily meetings—if you could be in one, you'd see we do so as a result of our advance planning. When you say that, I visualize charts all over the office, but we don't need them. We're on top of the job, so my answer is a qualified *yes*. But we do it informally as a matter of course.

These meetings last from thirty or forty-five minutes to an hour and a half. I find the holes in production, clarify problems, and assign responsibility. We talk about problems while they are fresh in our minds. I make assignments and take corrective action.

We have production reports that go weekly to headquarters so they are on top of what we're doing, too. We know where we stand all the time.

It takes daily hammering at the individual manager. We also have more long-range plans. Once a week we have a presentation on costs. We have a discussion, I make assignments, and we have a little ranting and raving.

Interviewer: Oh?

Dictator: Yeah, you know how it is. We discuss time-phase budgets, unit-cost budgets, and total-cost budgets. I let the people leave the meetings knowing what they must do. They have their assignments for the day. Also, as a result, they recognize their own problems—you know, why didn't I take care of that, hope it doesn't come up. So they assign themselves, too, so it won't come up in the next meeting.

I have a very rigid system of controls, all inviolable.

Interviewer: You seem to have a dynamic, forceful approach. How did you arrive at the operational philosophy you've described?

Dictator: I spent twenty years with Lockheed. So did my boss. And his superior's boss came from there too. These guys are really top managers. You know how we all got here?

Interviewer: Self-perpetuation?

Dictator: Yes, you could call it that I guess. Sure, he went back to Lockheed and hired several of us. You can't blame him for that. He knew what was needed and how we all operate.

Interviewer: Is what you described the general philosophy of Lockheed?

Dictator: I could talk for days about that. Sure, but it's more than a philosophy, it's techniques, too.[Described techniques, systems controls, etc.]

[Name of person] chopped people to hell when he came here. Started budgeting and follow-ups, insistence on performance. Are you familiar with Parkinson's Law?

Interviewer: Yes.

Dictator: He did it in reverse. Got rid of all the assistants-to, assistants to the assistants-to, all the non producers. Not just on the staff either. He got rid of them on the line. We had to make peace with the community. Cut out so many people they thought we were getting ready to move to Canada or something.

Interviewer: Really cut, huh?

Dictator: I didn't mention quality. In our meetings we review quality statistics—measure the number of defects, check receiving inspection, check rejections, scrap, and attrition.

Interviewer: Why were you sent here? Any special reason?

Dictator: That's a loaded question. [discussed personal occupational situation] I'm not too much on public relations. I'm in there on production.

Interviewer: How about public relations?

Dictator: The community can be semidamned as far as I'm concerned! I wasn't here when the plant first opened. Of course, that's another matter. But I'll tell you one thing, I don't run a basket case like some other plants were in the past. Some had a complete basket case on their hands.

Interviewer: Basket case?

Dictator: Yes, no procedural control, no discipline.

Interviewer: Discipline?

Dictator: I said discipline! [pounded the table] The boss says PR be damned—up to the point of getting in trouble. We don't want any complaints. He doesn't care how we handle it as long as there are no problems. Doesn't even ask.*

Interviewer: What really motivates you? Are you concerned for the welfare of your company, your own welfare, or both?

Dictator: Well, now, that's tough. I'll try to be honest, but how can you know you are for sure? I've always run my job as if it's my own business. My boss said when I came here he wouldn't have to worry about the plant. I try to offset my faults with my sterling qualities. I like my work and really dig in.

Interviewer: You work hard, don't you?

Dictator: Yes, but I never believed long hours, as such, would impress anybody. [got up and paced back and forth in the office] You know, I always thought if you performed you would progress, but in the last five to seven years I've realized you have to keep your face and name out in front too. I know one guy who was really good at telling the boss how well he did, and he really moved ahead—about 50 percent due to his skill in getting along with people. Others with much more ability haven't done nearly so well.

Interviewer: Why did it take you so long to recognize performance alone wasn't enough?

Dictator: I wish I knew. I learned it little by little and then all of a sudden it hit me. I bet a lot of people don't recognize it, do they?

Interviewer: Lots of them don't.

Dictator: Well, I guess I'm concerned for the company's welfare and mine too. They're the same mostly. [described self-interest and company interest accurately]

---

*Public relations were excellent in spite of these comments.

Interviewer: Yes, you're right. To what extent do you rely on unofficial actions, and end runs instead of the direct approach.

Dictator: I don't follow you.

Interviewer: Do you always do things directly or do you have to grease the skids occasionally—like get someone to see your boss first and prepare him in advance for something?

Dictator: I go direct. Why not?

Interviewer: We assumed you did, since your firm is quite objective, isn't it?

Dictator: Objective? My God, yes! [pounded the desk] Aren't they all?

Interviewer: No, unfortunately many are not. [explained lack of objectivity in many firms]

Dictator: Well I'll be damned! [threw a pen across the desk violently for emphasis] I never even considered it. We are, and Lockheed was too.

This interview gives a picture of a typical, highly skilled Dictator operating in a highly objective company. The managerial approach follows the classic examples of the dictatorial manager.[1]

This manager operates with stated formal objectives, many of which are established by the corporate headquarters. He also sets objectives and the plant operation is permeated with the emphasis on procedures, goals, and budgets. He has a rigid system of controls which he emphasizes are "inviolable." His daily meetings are designed to check on results, to set new objectives, and to review budgets. Consequently, this is a very rigid and formalized operation.

The emphasis on planning, provision of flexibility for the unexpected, and the use of some highly technical methods of control and measurement indicates the refinement of the plant operation.

This manager thinks of employee motivation in terms of follow-up and corrective action. The emphasis is on production and measurable results. The reasoning seems to be that setting objectives and following up daily will motivate the managers to produce the required results.

Communications are mostly one-way, from the top down, and consideration of the employees' feelings wasn't mentioned.

This dictatorial management approach was learned in another major company recognized for this approach, a company whose management team is admired. This Dictator, some of his supervisors, and peers were hired from the other company to clean up this portion of the company. They have been successful in making a measurable improvement in company operations.

The objectivity of the Dictator and his preoccupation with results is indicated by his attitude toward the community which "can be semidamned." The company does not rely on the community for sales outlets; rather, the inverse is true—the community relies on the company for employment of its citizens. The attitude toward the community is therefore objective, though hardly altruistic. As stated previously, however, public relations are excellent and the stated attitudes may be somewhat at variance with the plant's overall attitude toward the community.

The remarks concerning the inverse use of Parkinson's Law indicate the preoccupation with results and production and the apparent lack of concern for people. This law holds that an organization's rate of growth will increase at a predictable rate even though no more productive work is accomplished. The Dictator's comments refer to releasing people who were hired as a result of this law; that is, firing unnecessary people.

The Dictator briefly but vehemently emphasized the importance of discipline. He apparently assumed that the researchers (or anyone else) were well aware of the need for total discipline of employees.

This Dictator was aware of his own self-interest and company interest although he had not thought of them formally in those terms. His self-interest was constructive, and, therefore, was generally synonymous with company interests. The results he obtained were also believed to be in the best interests of the company since in this highly objective company self-interest is equated with company interest.

Of particular significance are the statements concerning his lack of perception in recognizing that production alone does not guarantee promotability. His recognition of the importance of social skills (and adapting to company expectations) came "suddenly" after many years of management experience. This lack of perception is the rule rather than the exception. This Dictator was concerned for others who had not developed it.

Unofficial actions or *end runs* were completely foreign to this manager since he had worked only in highly objective companies. This is reemphasized in his explosive reaction to questions on objectivity. He assumed that all organizations were objective. The degree of objectivity he was familiar with would doubtlessly be equally shocking to managers in most major companies.

This Dictator and his company are highly successful, and he is obviously an intelligent, highly skilled, and effective manager. A modification of this managerial approach is, however, worth considering.

Dictatorial Management at Amalgamated

Amalgamated is a large company with medium objectivity. It is bureaucratic and has a large supporting staff. It relies on unofficial actions, cliques, and adoptive nepotism and socio-nepotism. The management team, which is highly respected in the business world, includes all classifications of managers.

Amalgamated employees are required to adapt to company expectations, some of which are formal but many of which are informal and never stated. Since it is not totally objective, some employees find it very difficult to recognize the informal expectations and consequently to adapt to these expectations.

Although an old, established company, Amalgamated is growing rapidly. Consequently, promotions within the organization occur much more frequently than in industry as a whole.

An interview with Spivens, a foreman, and then with his supervisor showed that Spivens had a partial misconception about promotability.

We concentrate on results, and your ability to get these results controls in a large part how rapidly you can advance. When I came here, there were some serious problems, so I set about to correct them. The previous foreman wasn't very aggressive and was afraid to push the men. I think they expected me to be the same way. On my previous assignment things were different. And I operated in such a manner that I was respected and liked by my men. They cooperated, and we all worked together.

I took one look at this job and decided that I would have to jump in with both feet and start running things instead of letting the men do it. The assistant foremen weren't functioning, either. So I told Forney what I planned and he said "O. K."

Things got sticky for a while and I wasn't accepted by the men, but I wasn't running a popularity contest. They resisted me at first, but when our production went up, they gradually came around. They respected me at least, and now I think they like me a lot better. Forney has been hinting that if I keep getting improvement I'll probably get advanced before too long.

So to get ahead, you have to get the results they want. Sometimes I question that what they want is right, but we're judged by the statistical measurements. I try to give them what they want.

Forney, the section manager, was generally pleased with Spivens's accomplishments but had some reservations.

Spivens has done a remarkable job in a short period of time. He recognizes what's required and goes after it. I was concerned at first because he had a grievance shortly after he got there which was later dropped. He has shown he is capable of getting production, and the men and his assistant foremen don't resent him like they did at first.

His problem is he resents getting results he doesn't think are 100 percent right just to meet our reporting requirements, and it shows. He has to learn to accept things as they are. He makes a good appearance, is polished, and is basically very capable. People like him but he doesn't mingle too well with those higher up. He's not interested and apparently thinks he'll get ahead on the basis of his ability. I think I can get him promoted another level but if he's going any further, he had better straighten up.

Spivens was a capable foreman and had determined that one managerial approach will not fit all situations. He modified his accordingly from an apparent democratic approach on previous assignments to a dictatorial method to get the required results. This indicates his perception in recognizing that the question is often not which is the *best* approach, but which is the *most effective* approach for the circumstances. Spivens was also gradually modifying his dictatorial methods to democratic methods after the major problems had been corrected, demonstrating his flexibility.

He did not recognize the importance of favorably impressing his supervisors and relied on his accomplishments, which, as Forney pointed out, was a deterrent to unlimited promotability.

Spivens made these comments about Hill, the general plant manager:

Mr. Hill was the department head at [another plant] when I first met him, and I considered it probable that eventually he would become our general plant manager. I knew him fairly well, although I didn't work for him until he came here. He has always been aggressive.

He came here before I did, and the first week he came down and pointed out all the problems on my line and asked me what I was going to do about it, just as if I had been here forever and had created the problems. He knew as well as I did I was new on the job. He was right, there were many things that needed to be corrected, so I told him my plans and invited him to take a look at the line in a month or so. He seemed satisfied, and in a month or two I had things pretty well cleaned up. He knew it too and didn't come down on the line again until sometime later. You might say he got my attention.

Forney was pleased with the way Spivens handled Hill.

Hill came down right after Spivens was assigned to me and started chewing on him about results. I was concerned about how Spivens would handle him since he was new, but he looked Hill right in the eye and told him what he was going to do to effect corrections just as if he had caused the problems, and then with a straight face asked Hill to come back and check on him later. It shut Hill up pretty well. Spivens handled himself well. I like for my men to stand up for themselves. Upper management doesn't respect them if they scare easy, and it's a reflection on me. Spivens pitched in and cleaned things up, too.

The two preceding quotations show Hill's domineering approach which was designed, as Spivens pointed out, to get his attention. Stoddard, the operational staff manager, discussed this approach.

Hill is concerned only with results, and he uses the punishment and reward technique. If a foreman is doing well, he'll write him a memo to let him know he is aware of it. But if results slip, he'll get another memo pointing it out.

The men think he is watching them personally, but one of Hill's assistants screens the monthly reports and prepares the memos for Hill, so it's pretty routine. Hill knows what's going on generally, but he reviews the results reports before he says anything to anybody. He couldn't possibly know everything in infinite detail on a day-to-day basis; this operation is too complicated. Some of the men seem to think he does, which is his purpose, of course.

The lack of total objectivity and the willingness of Dictators to get results which are not necessarily in the best interest of the company are shown by the comments of Carr, a section manager.

Sometimes we have one thing emphasized, sometimes something else. Right now the company is concerned with maintenance expenses and a drive is underway to reduce them. We compete with our other plants, and ours has been a little higher.

Sometimes I think this company has gone crazy. All we hear is reduce maintenance. Well, we can all reduce it but we pay the price later. They don't seem to care how we do it. They just want it reduced. So everybody is scrambling to get it down. The problem is the same old thing—competition.

> We have to get better paper results than the other plants since that's what we're measured on. Actual results don't mean a thing. It's the paper results that count. When they put too much pressure on us, we have to find a way. The section managers and foremen who recognize what upper management really wants usually make out O. K., but those who try to run the lines properly get in trouble on results.

> I try to strike a happy medium. I have to meet the objectives, but I have to consider the end result too. The real objective is to get maintenance down and still keep things running. This is where real management comes in. You have to evaluate the situation and determine how you can reduce expenses the most with the least possible adverse effect. Those who cut back arbitrarily are going to be sorry later. I just hope they decide to emphasize something else like production before everything breaks down.

Amalgamated's dictatorial operational philosophy emphasizes measurable results to a greater degree than do other philosophies, with the exception of the opportunistic approach. These measurable results are the reports, measurements, and statistics relating to production, maintenance, quality control, and personnel losses.

This emphasis on paper measurements under a dictatorial philosophy in a company such as Amalgamated, which has only medium objectivity, causes the management team to concentrate on obtaining the expected results. Many managers recognize these results as not totally in the best interests of the company.[2]

The self-interest of the Dictator and other managers is not totally equated with company interest and is not totally constructive. Those managers, such as Spivens, with high company interest are not meeting the expectations of their company which requires more self-interest. Or they are disregarding the best interests of the company to have high promotability through obtaining the expected results.

We must avoid getting the cause and effect in juxtaposition. The situation as described is not the cause of the company's lack of objectivity, but the effect of it. If the general operational philosophy were objective, the insistence on obtaining results which are not necessarily in the best interests of the company would be greatly minimized.

We must also recognize that in a business as large and complex as Amalgamated total objectivity would be virtually impossible to attain because the combination of the self-interest of individual managers and the necessary internal competition tends to require measurable results. However, none of the members of the management team at Amalgamated (or any other company researched) had more than a vague recognition of the effects of objectivity or the lack of it on their organization and on themselves personally. It is obvious that the top executives, who should prefer almost total objectivity in their own self-interest, do not recognize the importance of objectivity or perhaps even consider it nonexistent.

The explanation for this apparent lack of perception is that many managers have devoted their careers to one company or to companies with a similar degree of objectivity and are consequently not in a position to make a meaningful comparison. In addition, as mentioned earlier, the managers in lower levels of supervision are too naive to recognize the corporate subculture as it really operates, and the highest-level managers are too far from the actual operations and are often *protected* by their employees. That is, they are told only what the employees think they want to hear. In the companies investigated, the middle-management people were the only strata of management on which the researchers could rely for valid overall evaluations.

Ayers, the department head, recognized some of Amalgamated's operational problems under a Dictator.

> The emphasis on results is not all good or all bad. Without such emphasis we couldn't operate as efficiently as we do. We have to temper this emphasis with consideration for the actual end results. I attempt to do this through interpretation of our measurable results, both as submitted to higher management and as directives for my section heads.

Dictatorial Management at Wildcat

Wildcat is an independent oil company with low objectivity. It is a nongrowth company controlled by a Manipulator and promotability is not a primary consideration since promotions occur infrequently.

Fielding, the computer supervisor in the company's accounting department, explained his dictatorial approach.

> When I assumed my position, the programs were inadequate and were designed in the main for a segmented operation. I set up the plans for our present coordinated and centralized information flow and gave my programmers and operators their assignments. Then I rode . . . [them] until we got this mess straightened out, which took over a year to make any real progress. I let one programmer go, and one of the unit record operators quit. And after that we made progress fairly rapidly. Summers turned it over to me to run the way I wanted to. We have a good operation now, and I gained a lot of experience. I'm looking around for a position with another company now. There's nowhere to go here.

Fielding's assistants, who were Technicians, were not receptive to Fielding's dictatorial approach. A computer attendant and programmer expressed their views:

> We got along pretty well back when we had unit record equipment and accounting machines, but after we got the 1401 we had some trouble. That's when Mr. Fielding was placed in charge of our operation.
>
> Some of us were disappointed that we weren't selected, but we accepted it and nobody resigned. The others might have resented it more if one of us had been promoted. I suppose Mr. Fielding was better qualified, anyway. He had experience that we all lacked, and he did finally design our present system. He's good at systems analysis.
>
> He's tough, though. He fired one of our programmers for incompetency. Another assistant quit some time later due to the pressure. He's done a good job all and all and he's O.K.

Another assistant was not as complimentary:

> He's efficient. I'll grant you that. But he's cold and calculating and all he cares about is integrated procedures with maximum output from

minimum core, which requires highly refined programs. He goes around saying, "garbage in, garbage out," which refers to the purity of his damn input.

He fired one of my friends who was a qualified programmer, and he pushes everybody. Summers lets him do it. It wasn't always like this around here.

Fielding was the only Dictator at Wildcat, and whether this was a continuing or a flexible operational philosophy was not determined. It is possible that this approach was used only to improve an inefficient operation.

Dictatorial Management at Diversified

Diversified is a large, nationally known company which has high objectivity. It consequently does not rely on cliques, unofficial actions, and adoptive nepotism and socionepotism to the degree that is true of Amalgamated. As do many similar companies, it has a dictatorial operational philosophy.

Stone, a foreman, discussed conditions at Diversified under its present Dictator as compared with conditions under the previous vice president-operations, who was an Abdicator.

The only way to get ahead in Diversified is on ability. They consider your qualifications, and the most capable man gets the advancement, which is the way it should be.

I like working here a lot better than I did before Mr. Hopkins·took over. Before, there was a lack of coordination. We just sort of muddled around without any real sense of direction. Now we have everything lined out for us and we know exactly what we are expected to do. We run on our schedules, and I coordinate inventories with the other foremen. So it's a smooth operation.

Mr. Hopkins really straightened everything out. He pushes everybody, and we all have to produce. I mean this is no easy job, but it is a lot better feeling that you are accomplishing something. I'd rather work hard than be frustrated not knowing exactly what I'm supposed to do or how to do it.

We have meetings three times a week to coordinate our work. I don't get to go but my boss and all the higher levels do. Mr. Hopkins gives everybody instructions, and they come out and give the foremen our instructions.

I think this is a good place to work, and I like the people I work with. Mr. Hopkins doesn't get too close to us at my level, but after all, he's awfully busy. He works as hard or harder than the rest of us.

Stone is pleased with the working conditions and the sense of accomplishment which he feels was made possible by Hopkins, whom he never failed to address as "Mister." He expresses his approval principally for Hopkins rather than for his immediate supervisor or the management team as a whole. He seems to view Hopkins as the principal guiding force of the organization. His defense of Hopkins being too busy to "get close" to the foremen is an indication of his own desire for Hopkins' personal recognition.

Stone's attitude was representative of the other line foremen in this organization, all of whom viewed Hopkins as the directing force of the operation, due largely to the comparison with the previous top executive.

Rodgers, the general foreman, shared the view of other managers at his level. Their attitude contrasts sharply with that of the line foremen.

Every Monday, Wednesday, and Friday at 10 o'clock sharp come hell or high water, we have a coordination meeting which usually lasts until noon. We analyze our current production in relation to our objectives, analyze our inventory control situation, review all of our cost budgets, and get into everything in infinite detail.

All this time we have most of management out of the operations where we should be. We have to justify our production and any problems we might have, and it can get agonizing. Hopkins takes as much time and puts as much emphasis on very minor items as he does on major ones. He lays it on us good about everything and anything. I tell you that man is a perfectionist. He's capable and he's a fine manager, but he runs everything himself. The only initiative we show is in preparing for the meetings so we don't get in trouble. This takes a lot of time, thought, and effort which could better be spent in improving our operations.

We do compare favorably with [another plant], and I feel we have an efficient operation. We all work together and there's very little friction. It's those meetings that tear me up. When I leave them, I'm usually so mad I don't give a damn if the job gets done or not.

Hopkins justifies his managerial approach in this way:

I feel a firm must operate with established goals and procedures which permit up-to-the-minute evaluation of our position. We have our objectives which I see my people meet; and, of course, we have our formalized reports. I also have productivity meetings several times a week in which we resolve any problems, and these are instrumental in obtaining our production quotas.

The dictatorial approach in Diversified is highly successful, but the attitudes toward it vary considerably at the various levels of supervision. The lower levels are generally pleased, but this is based on a comparison and their relative inexperience. The middle managers who are more experienced recognize the success of the operation and agree with the general approach. They are, however, in disagreement with the emphasis on follow-up activities. This is usually the case when dictatorial approaches take a great deal of time which managers feel could be better spent in managing rather than in justifying.

At Diversified the lower levels of management were too inexperienced to recognize the true effects of the managerial approach. The top manager was equally unaware of the results of his continued dictatorial methods after the *clean-up* had been accomplished.

The dictatorial approaches at Amalgamated and Diversified had different effects because of the differences in the companies' objectivity. At Diversified, a more objective company than Amalgamated, the self-interest of the Dictator was equated to company interest and the results he obtained were in the best interests of his company.

In Amalgamated the self-interest of the Dictator was not totally equated to company interest and was in part nonconstructive since the results sought were not always in the company's best interests.

Yet here we have a paradox in that the less objective company even with a dictatorial upper-management approach had more concern for people. The objectivity at Diversified was directed to production with little concern for the personal feelings of people, and as with the Dictator interviewed at the beginning of this chapter, motivation consisted almost entirely of insisting on results.

The lack of objectivity in Amalgamated could be inaccurately considered in terms of more empathy. The lack of concern at Diversified for people is in effect a form of nonobjectivity since motivated people can better produce the results expected in an objective company.

Total objectivity was lacking in both companies. Diversified had a more efficient operation, but employee morale at Amalgamated was better.

Summary

The dictatorial approach can and often is highly successful, especially for a short period when a relaxed operation needs marked and immediate improvement. A continued dictatorial approach, however, often results in loss of human resources, as occurred at Wildcat, and over a period may result in lower production.[3]

The Dictator's approach is not nearly as effective as that of the Executive who considers what methods are appropriate for the time, person, and circumstances.

Although companies with a dictatorial operational philosophy have many Dictators, industry in general reports that this classification has fewer members than the other classifications.

Literature Cited

1. For a similar description of a dictatorial philosophy, see Chris Argyris, "Leadership Pattern in the Plant," *Harvard Business Review*, XXXII, 1 (January-February, 1954), 64-75.

2. Rensis Likert speaks of the cost of authoritarian pressures which, although effective in increasing productivity over the short run, increases the costs of the human assets—hostilities increase, loyalty declines, and motivation decreases. Management can expect their better personnel to leave the company. See Likert, "Measuring Organizational Performance," *Harvard Business Review,* XXXVI (March - April, 1958), pp. 41-50.

3. Ibid.

10 : the opportunist

The Opportunist—the intelligent, striving, self-oriented manager whose results are attained for his own benefit and not for his company's—is found in many organizations. This breed of executive thrives in nonobjective companies that leave him room to maneuver.

Interview with an Opportunist

Interviewer: How is the job progressing?

Opportunist: Fine, fine, I just came up from the plant and we have her humming along. I got the month-ending reports this morning, and we're still leading on about everything. We're way out in front with a 1482 on [a major index] compared with a general plant average of around 1000. So we're doing O.K. I wanted to break 1500, but I think we can make it this month. If we do, they'll probably reevaluate our coefficients.

Interviewer: Why will they reevaluate?

Opportunist: Well, if we break 1500, we'll be 50 percent above our established standards using the present units and a base of 1000, so they'll increase the unit requirements and adjust back to a base of 1000 using our output. What it means is we'll be meeting the new standards at 1000, but the others will be below. And their objective will be to match our output and reach the objective of 1000.

Interviewer: So you have a head start.

Opportunist: Sure. But I'll be trying to go over the new standard.

Interviewer: Can you?

Opportunist: Maybe. Not as much as before, though. We have most of the slack out of it now.

Interviewer: How did you manage to go so far over the established objective?

Opportunist: By wanting to mostly and finding a way.

Interviewer: What way?

Opportunist: That's rather complicated. See, we were rocking along and our output in the plant was in a favorable comparative position when I took over, but I wanted to make as much improvement as I could. I know from past experience people can produce more if they are shown the way, so I set to work on it—finding ways to improve and encouraging them to increased productivity.

Interviewer: How do you go about encouraging them?

Opportunist: Well, the first thing is to let them know you expect it. I approach them on taking a competitive attitude, trying to outproduce the others, and stimulate them to want to find ways to increase output.

Interviewer: How do you stimulate them?

Opportunist: I take a personal interest in each phase of the operation. And when one of the section heads, for example, improves, I recognize him for it. On the other hand, if one is not producing, I let him know about that, too.

Interviewer: Reward and punishment?

Opportunist: Certainly. If a man can produce for me, I take care of him. If he can't, there are always those who can.

Interviewer: How do you reward your better managers?

Opportunist: Money. I give them raises. Recognition. I report their accomplishments in the best possible light in the [company publication]. Then I take care of the ones who I feel are real comers by bringing them along in the organization.

Interviewer: Promotions?

Opportunist: Yes, I give good reports on those who are deserving. They earn it. I have several men with me who worked for me at [another plant].

Interviewer: You brought them with you?

Opportunist: No, not when I came. They joined me later as openings occurred.

Interviewer: These men had proved previously that they could produce?

Opportunist: Yes, they're good men and fit well into the organization. They know how to get the results.

Interviewer: How does the punishment part work?

Opportunist: Just the opposite, really. I work with them and try to develop those who don't produce. It's a problem of motivation, mostly. I do the best I can for them and some come along quite well. A few just don't have it.

Interviewer: Don't have it?

Opportunist: No. Unfortunately some just don't fit in properly and can't seem to adjust to the job requirements.

Interviewer: Requirements?

Opportunist: Yeah, they just want to plug along, won't really get with it and find a way to meet our production requirements. A few sort of passively resist our efforts at improved operations.

Interviewer: Oh?

Opportunist: I have to get rid of one occasionally. Usually transfer them to a less demanding position.

Interviewer: How, specifically, do your better managers outproduce the others?

Opportunist: Here again it's principally a matter of wanting to. They dig in and push harder. They are also paid to think, to find ways to improve. The thing is, they also take care of the people under them who can produce. So it becomes a matter of competition within our own organization. They become quite skilled at negotiating with other departments on inventories and work-flow schedules. They make sure we're not held up waiting on some other department to meet schedules. So our work flows smoothly. Then we have good relations with maintenance, so we aren't down very often or very long. A delay due to breakdown can hurt you quick.

Interviewer: Why don't the other managers do the same things?

Opportunist: Lack of aggressiveness, I'd say. They aren't motivated enough to work at it and figure the angles.

Interviewer: Angles?

Opportunist: Well, by that I mean the ramifications involved with a complicated process like ours. It's not enough to just know the technical production job. You have to be in a position to control your inventories, for example. Also, remember, your production workers have to be motivated. They have to want to produce.

Interviewer: How do you motivate them?

Opportunist: The same, generally, as with the management people. They have their little gripes and things that they want, so we help them as much as we can.

Interviewer: Reward exceptional performers?

Opportunist: Yes, some. But also the group. If you are fair and considerate of the group, they tend to encourage the slower workers.

Interviewer: Group motivation?

Opportunist: I guess. We try to keep them happy. If we have dissenting voices, we try to work with them and bring a little pressure to bear. I pull the assistant foremen up to my office occasionally and have a little chat with them.

Interviewer: Motivate them?

Opportunist: I don't mince any words, if that's what you mean. I'm nice about it, though. Try to get them to recognize the errors of their ways, as it were.

Interviewer: What motivates you personally? You seem to work pretty hard at your job.

Opportunist: I guess I like to compete and try to do a better job for the company than others at my level.

Interviewer: You are interested in the welfare of the company?

Opportunist: Oh yes, I live and breathe this company, and so I do the best I can for it. This is really a fine company, one of the best in my estimation.

Interviewer: What about your own interests?

Opportunist: Oh, I'm ambitious, if that's what you mean. I've been fortunate in being able to produce for the company so they have taken care of me pretty well. I'm one of the youngest plant managers, which makes me feel pretty good.

Interviewer: You feel you have been promotable due to your excellent results in the past?

Opportunist: Yes, partly, but it takes more than that. You have to figure the angles too. I was offered a promotion a few years ago that I turned down since it didn't offer a real chance to show what you could do. I'm glad I did, too. [Name] took it and he's still there. No, it takes more than just pure results. You have to consider the less obvious things.

Interviewer: For instance?

Opportunist: Well, I don't know; it's hard to explain. I guess results are most of it.

Interviewer: You worked for [a higher-level Opportunist] previously, didn't you?

Opportunist: Yes. Fine man. Capable executive.

Interviewer: Did your performance under him influence your selection for your present position?

Opportunist: Oh, a little maybe. We're judged on our basic capabilities, so adequate performance is important.

Interviewer: I thought perhaps he'd selected you since you worked for him before and you seem to get along O.K.

Opportunist: Selections are made on the basis of evaluations [discussed formal appraisal methods]. I doubt [he] had too much to do with it. That [town] was an interesting place [discussed it at length].

Interviewer: How objective do you think your company is? That is, how interested is it in its own welfare?

Opportunist: Oh, I'd say almost completely objective. We all work together and I'd say we have the interests of the company at heart. This is a good company, like I said.

Interviewer: Do you normally take a direct approach to things, or do you have to resort to other methods occasionally to get things done?

Opportunist: If I get what you mean, I'd say we use the direct approach mostly.

Interviewer: Few end runs?

Opportunist: This is a good company, and we work together.

Interviewer: I understand there has been some problem with quality controls recently. High reject rates.

Opportunist: Uh huh.

Interviewer: Do you have specific plans to improve this phase of the operations?

Opportunist: Well, you have to view this in connection with the whole. For example, while it is possible for rates to increase, when you have high productivity the cost of the rate diminishes. So you still have a more economical operation with a little higher reject rate.

Interviewer: I understood that the rate increased appreciably.

Opportunist: Oh, not really. I'd say it's within reasonable levels.

Interviewer: Isn't there a concentrated effort being made to reduce it, though?

Opportunist: Well, we watch these things of course, and I anticipate there will be a marked improvement soon.

Interviewer: How does your rate compare with other comparable facilities?

Opportunist: Oh, we're doing O.K. And of course our production is superior.

Interviewer: Isn't your rate a little higher, though?

Opportunist: Look, I was told to cooperate with you, and I've done it. But I'm not permitted to give out confidential statistics. You've been poking around here and getting some superficial information you can't analyze except in relation to the whole.

Interviewer: Yes, perhaps you're right. Looking at the company as a whole, what would you say the operational philosophy is?

Opportunist: Well, I'd say we are all directed toward doing the best we can for the company in general and maintaining or increasing our competitive position in the industry. And I'd say we are doing quite well.

Interviewer: You mean your company works toward common goals and its teamwork is largely responsible for its success?

Opportunist: Yes, and I might add my own thoughts on that. I enjoy working here, and it gives me a feeling of accomplishment. Our discussion has been thought provoking, and I think it's good for us to sit back and talk about the business. It gives me an opportunity to consider our operation. I think we get so wrapped up in our duties it's good to get away from it for a while. Listen, if I can help you in any way, you remember the door's open.

The information obtained in this interview is more informative when we recognize what was inferred rather than what was said. The Opportunist was pleased with his remarkable improvement in output which had increased about 50 percent and which he believed might result in a reevaluation of the measurement plan. This would doubtlessly result in a great deal of recognition for the Opportunist. No information about the rate of rejects was mentioned, however. How popular the Opportunist was with his peers is also unknown.

The Opportunist motivated his employees with rewards and punishments. The rewards were salary advances and increased promotability. The punishments were transfers to less desirable jobs and possibly ended careers.

The principal expectancy was described as "finding a way" to increase output. Considerable pressure was placed on the employees to find these ways. They were also "paid to think," which meant negotiating with other departments for a smooth flow of work.[1]

The perspectives of the employees of this Opportunist were somewhat different than his. One employee described the situation in this way:

Most of us knew what to expect when we found out [the Opportunist] had been made [job title], but that doesn't mean we were prepared for it. We have several of them around like [the Opportunist], but it's my impression he's the worst. He came around glad-handing everybody and talking about "that old competitive spirit" and "getting the job done." He said we had to all "pull together" for our mutual advantage. Then he started pushing us for more output.

I'll give him credit for one thing. He never did tell us specifically how we were to get it. The fact is, he doesn't give a damn how you get it as long as you don't get him in trouble. Some of the section heads and foremen caught on right away. And some took a little longer to learn the hard way. We started stretching the rules. We give the men on the line privileges they never had before as long as they produce, and that's something I wouldn't care to go into.

We learned how to put the screws to the other departments too. That brings our production up. But it automatically means that the other departments that depend on us have their production go down. How do you think they feel about us?

The supporting departments were not at all happy with the situation. One manager described how the Opportunist's methods affected his department.

We're caught in a vice. They insist on immediate and preferential treatment totally without regard to proper priorities, and we give it to them. So sure they do better than the others. Who wouldn't? There's not a thing we can do about it either, because if we don't give them what they want, they hold up delivery on the other end. And then we are bogged down on the rest of our work flow. It's blackmail, pure and simple.

You try to get something done with [the Opportunist], and he's oh so concerned trying to help you. He always has a reason for any delays on his part. What he does is find a semilogical reason why it's your own fault. And if you try to get back at him, he finds a way to cause you more trouble than you'd believe. He's smooth; I'll tell you that. Always cordial and friendly as he cuts your throat.

I don't blame his people. I know they are forced into it. But if you hadn't known some of them before, you'd think they're about as bad as he is. He imported that [name] too. He's another one.

The Opportunist *imported* several of his previous employees who had learned their lessons well and were considered to be the same type of managers. Another employee referred to this in these observations:

He brought [name] in from another plant, and it looked like he wanted him since he can get the output like [the Opportunist] wants. I question this now though. I think it's possible [name] knows too much about [the Opportunist] , and he feels safer with him under his thumb. You hear rumors and don't know what to believe, but I think that has something to do with it. It's pretty well accepted that they were involved in a situation of questionable ethics.

Most of the Opportunist's peers believed that the Opportunist too had attained his position because of adoptive nepotism—a situation which, if true, the Opportunist denied or minimized.

The Opportunist also "motivated" his employees ranking as low as assistant foreman by talking with them in his office. One assistant foreman said this:

I was told to go to his office, so I knew I was in for it. He had me sit down and gave me a cigarette while he established rapport. Then he went into how my family was and seemed concerned about my personal life and my welfare. He asked me about the job and what I was doing and encouraged me to think about it and patted me on the shoulder and walked me to the door.

I didn't think it was too bad until I had time to mull it over. What he really said was if I didn't play ball I'd get fired. That's what it meant.

The Opportunist seemed to regard his company highly and said he thought it was objective. He was in all probability aware that this was not true since he helped contribute to the marked lack of objectivity.

He was obviously reluctant to discuss the reasons for his own high degree of promotability. After evading the question, he concluded that the results he obtained made him promotable.

The Opportunist was more than reluctant to discuss the high rate of rejects that accompanied his increased production and attempted to justify them as being at "reasonable" levels. This became "confidential" while production statistics were discussed openly. Further questioning on this subject almost terminated the interview.

Opportunism at Wildcat

The opportunism in Wildcat was not restricted to Hawkins and Applewhite. Schmidt, the president, rated as an Executive with equal self-interest and company interest, was originally an Opportunist. He and his partner, Jake, created the company through lease operations as reported in the chapter on the Dictator. They agreed to drill on each lease within 30 days but "couldn't have drilled but one damn well."

The history of the petroleum business is based in a large part on opportunism. The Ranger oil boom is representative of the industry and the opportunism which prevailed.

Ranger's discovery-well was drilled by Frank Champion in October, 1917. The John McCleskey is located south of the city near the Lone Star plant and just west of Highway 80. Mr. Champion recalls the events of that day:

> I brought in the first producer in the Ranger Field with Harv Wells, my tooldresser. Harv had little experience, and I taught him to dress tools on that well. The first I knew she was coming in was when I felt the sand and it was oily—we did that frequently, you know. Well, Harv had gotten the ropes all balled up and I went over to help him straighten them out, and she blew in. So I ran over and took a couple of turns on the screw and headed for town. Went to the telephone office on Main Street and called Wagner [drilling contractor] in Strawn and told him she had come in.

> It was a Saturday afternoon in October. My friend Dick Hodges, the Chevrolet dealer, drove up and down Main hollering at everybody that the McCleskey had blown in. It had been real dry. So the farmers weren't doing much anyway, and everybody for miles around headed for the McCleskey. I put Harv to taking matches off everybody because I didn't want her to catch fire.

> Well, she flowed free for about four weeks. We dug pits to hold the flow until they got the tanks set up. John McCleskey had a herd of fine cattle, and 18 of them drank oil and died. And we had to pay for them. At the end of four weeks, she was flowing at 450 barrels a day and Wagner told me to go deeper. But he had cut the rope and taken my string of tools to another location. I rigged a new string and got her started while Wagner wiped the oil out of my face so I could see—spraying all over, you know, oil everywhere. I got her started and went down 7 more feet and the flow came to 1,750 barrels.[2]

The Ranger boom was created through the efforts of John M. Gholson, a prominent merchant in Ranger, and other businessmen who prevailed on W. K. Gordon to finance drilling operations in the Ranger area. Gordon, the superintendent for Texas Pacific Coal Company with mining operations in Thurber (some 16 miles east of Ranger), had been interested in the oil potential. Through his efforts, his company financed the exploration in exchange for rights to the major portion of the Ranger field.

The first well was drilled by George and John Dunkle on the Nannie Walker farm, north of the city. They hit gas but no oil, and the gas was permitted to flow free. The well blew in later, but not until four others were producing.

With the discovery-well, the boom was on. The population of Ranger increased within six months from 800 to 6,000. Within a year the population was up to 25,000.

The fourth producer was drilled on the Hagaman Ranch, east of the city. J. H. Ervin, a resident of Ranger, lived on family ranch property adjacent to the Hagaman Ranch and shared the disappointment of many others whose wells were nonproducers or low producers as was his. Mr. Ervin described the boom days for us.[3]

> Ranger was a quiet little town before the boom, but then people came in from everywhere. Drillers, contractors, tooldressers, roustabouts, carpenters, teamsters, and the crooks [and] gamblers . . . They began throwing up shacks everywhere and pretty soon we had a shack town. Things got a little rough. Most everybody was out to get rich quick. Everybody was money mad.

> They started hauling in equipment from everywhere and Main Street was a steady stream of horses, mules, oxen, wagons and equipment. When it rained, Main Street was all mud. I saw a team of horses drown one day. Bogged down in the mud and couldn't get them out.

> Cost you 2 bits or 50¢ to cross the street on a sled pulled by a team. I saw a lady once refuse to pay it. She stepped off the boardwalk and sunk up to her hips. We pulled her out, and she paid her way across.

The arriving mass of humanity included the landmen, leasemen, oil-company scouts, and others who sought opportunities for quick riches. Many sought their fortunes in the same manner as Schmidt and Jake of Wildcat. Schmidt recalls:

You may not think what we done was total ethical, and it wouldn't be now. But it was mild compared to what was going on. Some of them would sign up leases after the bank closed and give the landowner a check for money they didn't have. Then they'd have the rest of the weekend to sell the lease to someone else for more money. Could make a lot of money that way. If they got caught, chances were they got off anyway. Too much confusion, murders and crime, to get too upset about it. Me and Jake was downright noble compared to most. Nobody ever lost a cent on us, anyway.

They had a bunch of real oilmen in there too, come from all over. Bunch of them stayed on after the boom too. I thought you had to be a Pennsylvania Dutchman to be in the business before Ranger . . . .

The immensity of the Ranger boom can be seen by a comparison with the Gold Rush of 1849 which produced only $10 million. In 1920 the Ranger field produced oil with a value of $100 million.

The total amount paid for leases at Ranger would have required production of over 500 million barrels. This was quite a gamble when the output for the United States at the time was less than 350 million barrels.

Schmidt was generally aware of the optimism which prevailed during the Ranger and Hogtown booms:

Hell, that's why me and Jake got with Tooler. We made it, but we had enough sense to keep it too and do something with it. Any damn fool could see it couldn't last forever. We lost a little, but not much, when she fizzled out. That's when we got with Tooler and started in to learn to be businessmen instead of prospectors.

The Ranger boom epitomized the opportunism. Citizens of New York were victimized for an estimated $500 million in oil frauds in one year, largely on Ranger speculations. Schmidt said:

Sure, Wildcat was started on speculation and worse. But you damn sure don't hear nobody complaining about it that ever worked for us or any other oil company, except maybe because they didn't do it too. Anybody don't like it can kiss my foot.

Opportunism at Amalgamated

There are Opportunists in Amalgamated but as in most companies many are detected at the lower levels and are separated from the company. Those who are permitted to *resign* are normally considered by their supervisors to have "exercised poor judgment" or simply to have been involved in situations which are not tolerated. Some were unable to obtain the desired results from their employees because of their opportunism. At Amalgamated, opportunism is recognized but is not defined. Few of the employees recognize that those Opportunists who are dismissed share a common trait.

Several managers discussed one Opportunist who was dismissed. Wade's comments are recorded:

> John was intelligent and aggressive, and we all thought he would progress in the business. I still say he was capable, but he got off on the wrong foot. He was having trouble with results. And at first, everybody thought it was due to circumstances and some of the men who are known personnel problems. John would look you straight in the eye and explain his problems with such sincerity you had to believe him. He always made a point of being an attentive listener and he made everyone feel he thought they were the greatest.

> The only trouble was he was lying. He stretched the truth on both ends and bent it in the middle. The men recognized him for what he was, and they wanted no part of him. He was modifying reports too, but it was never proved. It's a shame. I guess there was something wrong with him.

Another foreman, a friend of John, didn't agree:

> I think John was railroaded. If higher management had stood behind him, he could have straightened things out. They sided with the men. John was trying to do a good job, and he was aggressive enough to dig

in and face his problems. He had to start over after they let him go, and he has a family. I think it's a rotten deal.

Forney, a section manager, had more details on the situation:

> I know what happened. It came out in a personnel meeting right afterwards. He was falsifying reports, which was proved, and his supervision of the men left something to be desired. He would tell them to do something, and if anything went wrong he'd tell his boss right in front of them that he told them to do something else. It's a wonder the men didn't do worse than report him. John was always thinking of himself and trying too hard to get ahead. He was intelligent, but that's pure stupidity.

A more serious case was reported by a higher-level manager, a situation which was common knowledge:

> Everybody knows about it, so there is no use in attempting to hide it. These situations occur infrequently, but I suppose they do happen in any company.
>
> Tim was taking kickbacks on supplies and had been for at least several years. He had involved some of his subordinates too. Then he started ordering supplies and diverting them. He also got into some other things it's better not to talk about. Some of the people who knew him well refuse to believe any of it. That's the pitiful part. You trust someone and know him for years and then find it out. It's all documented of course. We could have prosecuted, but we let him resign quietly to save the company the embarrassment.

Attempted falsification of reports is fairly common at Amalgamated.

> I can name a number of our former managers who I know were falsifying their production reports. It used to be more prevalent than it is now since we have better methods of checking. These guys would hide some of their reject cards and maintenance expense slips and maybe run in extra production unit cards. They would be suspected and maybe caught. And usually they were up to something else too, and sooner or later they'd get fired.

I know some of them who didn't get caught or did and lived through it. It sometimes depends on who your boss is. Some people get promoted for what others get fired for. Look at Templo.

Unethical practices are apparently prevalent in many companies. Dalton reported in his study of "Milo" an operational philosophy which included such practices as hiding and transferring inventories during inspections, setting up nonoperational departments, ignoring headquarters office directives, manufacturing special and costly products for executives, diverting supplies, openly repairing personal cars with company labor on company premises at company expense, diverting extremely large sums of money from one department to another to veil operations, and *paying off* executives with elaborate offices at considerable expense to keep them quiet and happy.[4]

Articles have appeared in various business periodicals lamenting the increasing dishonesty in industry and the necessity for more effective controls.[5] In most companies there is no totally effective way to combat dishonesty because of the many methods by which executives can be dishonest.

Although the operational philosophy at Amalgamated is designed to prevent or minimize open dishonesty, opportunism is not only often tolerated at the middle management and higher levels but is rewarded with promotability. Collins, a Noncontroversial Conformist, was promoted and replaced by Templo, an Opportunist. The operational philosophy was modified accordingly, as reported by a section manager.

As soon as Templo moved in, we were back on the results kick at any cost again just like we were under Hill [a Dictator], with one major difference. Under Hill we were expected to get the results honestly; although with as much pressure as he put on, some fudged a little. Now we're expected to get the results—period. Some of the managers just shrug it off and start doing what's expected. Others haven't learned yet, and I doubt anybody will stick their neck out trying to educate them. Of course there are some who never will get the message and others with inflexible standards of ethics who will end up in trouble.

The appointment of Templo, who was well known to many of the management team, was met with misgivings by all except those with opportunistic tendencies. A middle-management employee expressed his views:

> Templo is all right, and I was glad in a way he got the general plant manager job. Templo knows that you have to outproduce your competitors if you want to get ahead. And I've never been afraid of a little competition. With Templo we'll all pitch in and put this plant on the map again. It's good for all of us. He'll take care of you if you produce too. I think I'll move quicker under Templo than I would under Collins.

According to Forney, Parks, another Opportunist, was personally affected by the appointment of Templo.

> When they announced that Templo was coming back, I thought Parks would have a heart attack. Parks and Templo used to work together, and they didn't get along. Templo said he'd get Parks someday, and that day is here. He'll do it too.

Soon after Templo's appointment, Parks was off the job for an extended period because of peptic ulcers. No direct connection was substantiated, but Parks' friends believed it was related.

After Templo's appointment as general plant manager, a higher degree of opportunism was displayed by many managers, although certainly not by all. The increase in opportunism was the result of the managers' attempts to adapt to the corporate expectations.

Opportunism at Diversified

Diversified is so permeated with the dictatorial operational philosophy that opportunism is not a major consideration. The objectivity in the plant precludes open opportunism. Rodgers, classified as an Opportunist, displayed these tendencies, but because of the company's objectivity his opportunistic self-interest was of necessity directed principally toward company interest.

This is an example of controlled opportunism through an objective corporate environment.

Summary

The methods of Dictators and Opportunists are similar in that these approaches are used to obtain results. The dictatorial approach even generates opportunism when insistence on results is greater than the individual's capacity to produce. This approach can be effective in an objective environment. Opportunism, however, is seldom found in an objective environment because it is—in its blatant form—the antithesis of objectivity.

Opportunism is not in the best interests of any company and should be recognized and controlled through an objective operational philosophy, yet there may be more Opportunists in industry than there are Dictators. In 8 percent of the companies reporting from our survey of *Fortune's* 500, the Opportunists were outnumbered only by the Executives. Disregarding the Executive and Technician classifications, 15 percent of the major companies reported that they have more Opportunists than they have of any of the remaining classifications.

Literature Cited

1. Dill, Hilton, and Reitman, *The New Managers*, p. 239.

2. Interview with Mr. Frank Champion on October 15, 1967.

3. It is impossible to credit all those who provided the background information on the Ranger boom. Mr. Ervin as well as many others offered valuable information. Many citizens had firsthand experience during the boom. The abundant information available is considered to be general knowledge. Excellent references include *The Ranger Story*, published by the *Ranger Times*; Carl Coke Rister, *The Titan of the Southwest* (Norman: University of Oklahoma Press, 1949); and Boyce House, *Roaring Ranger, The World's Biggest Boom* (San Antonio, Texas: Naylor Company, 1951).

4. Dalton, *Men Who Manage.*

5. For example, see Thomas J. Murray, "The Case of the Disloyal Executive," *Dun's Review,* XC, No. 6 (December, 1967), 35.

11 : the noncontroversial conformist

The Noncontroversial Conformist—the friendly, sociable, compromising manager who seldom sticks his neck out—is generally found in all parts of industry. The exception to this is in the highly objective or authoritarian companies whose philosophies leave little room for this executive. But in bureaucratic organizations, he may be a successful manager.

Interview with a Noncontroversial Conformist

Interviewer: What is your operational philosophy? By that, I mean your approach to your management team.

Noncontroversial Conformist: Well, here . . . we work together. I believe in leading my people rather than driving them. We emphasize teamwork. Is that what you mean?

Interviewer: Yes. How do you lead your people?

Noncontroversial Conformist: Well, I don't know. It's rather complicated. Let me give you an example. When I assumed my present duties, our units per hour didn't compare favorably with the plant I'd just come from, and in my initial discussions with [my supervisor] and my department heads I discovered that slightly different procedures were used here. I wanted firsthand information, so I immediately arranged to make a tour of our whole plant.

Interviewer: What did you do on the tour?

Noncontroversial Conformist: I visited with all of my section managers in their offices so we could get acquainted, and asked a lot of questions. In these discussions I pointed out how we did certain things in [the

146

other plant] and asked their opinions. They were quite receptive to any suggestions I made.

Then I visited with the foremen on the line and talked with them and some of the men. I watched each operation and noted the differences as compared with [the other plant.]

Interviewer: You made suggestions to the foremen?

Noncontroversial Conformist: Oh, yes, but let me emphasize that these were *suggestions*. At this point I didn't give instructions since I was still not completely familiar with our operation. I just pointed out some of the differences and discussed my experiences and then asked that they consider some minor changes.

Interviewer: These were suggestions on minor changes?

Noncontroversial Conformist: Yes, relatively so. Of course a complex operation like ours is made up of many functions which combined make up the whole.

Interviewer: Could you give an example?

Noncontroversial Conformist: Let's see. Well, in the area of inventory control I explained a method of checks and balances which involves tagging [a major component] prior to assembly with an adhesive form segmented with perforations so at each stage a record can be maintained. We later adopted this system.

Interviewer: Yes.

Noncontroversial Conformist: And I suggested some rearrangements in the lines to facilitate more rapid assembly.

Interviewer: These were methods employed in the other plant?

Noncontroversial Conformist: Yes. They work very well too. Then there were several other similar things I suggested.

Interviewer: Now that you have been here for awhile how would you describe your operational philosophy?

Noncontroversial Conformist: We believe in a more or less scientific approach, and we have various training programs for our people. These stress such items as motivation, human relations in management, leadership qualities and that sort of thing. I encourage my managers to participate in these and learn as much as they can. We have a really fine program.

Interviewer: How are policy decisions reached, and how do you go about giving your people specific instructions?

Noncontroversial Conformist: We have meetings as the need arises which the upper-level managers attend. We have discussions, throw the problem out on the table and arrive at the best solution. Then, too, I schedule other meetings periodically. These are informative. They're designed to keep everybody aboard on items of interest. My staff people who specialize in certain areas make presentations on such things as new or revised quality-control procedures, cost accounting, inventory control and that sort of thing. We sometimes introduce procedural modifications in this way.

Interviewer: I see. Do you sometimes make specific recommendations yourself?

Noncontroversial Conformist: Yes, I do. Of course major changes originate either in R and D [Research and Development] or our procedural methods group, but the more routine operational considerations which affect the day-to-day operations are originated here.

Interviewer: What do you do with these?

Noncontroversial Conformist: I'm in close touch with [individual staff managers] and they make studies and prepare recommendations. I review these and we determine the most appropriate course of action and prepare instructions accordingly.

Interviewer: Your instructions to your department heads are based on these studies and recommendations?

Noncontroversial Conformist: Yes, in letter form usually and with various practices depending on the situation.

Interviewer: These are your duties and responsibilities then?

Noncontroversial Conformist: Principally, yes. Of course, I have a great deal of interdepartmental coordination. I attend a lot of meetings as the ranking member of my organization.

Interviewer: Is there interdepartmental rivalry? And do you take care of your department's interests?

Noncontroversial Conformist: Well, yes, certainly there is some rivalry, but it's friendly since we work toward a common objective. We do coordinate our activities in meetings and then there is less formal coordination on a day-to-day basis. I'm responsible for . . . [a peripheral staff organization] also.

Interviewer: Do you spend much time supervising their activities?

Noncontroversial Conformist: Not a great deal, usually only as related to operational considerations. They are well organized and it doesn't require a great deal of my attention.

Interviewer: I understand that due to your previous experience you were assigned to [a special project] and were gone for several months.

Noncontroversial Conformist: Seven weeks, actually. Yes, it was very interesting meeting with [the other people] and working together. Sort of a broadening experience.

Interviewer: Did you have a replacement here?

Noncontroversial Conformist: No, it wasn't necessary. I kept in touch as well as I could on any matters of considerable importance. I came in a few weekends too, so it worked out all right.

Interviewer: How were instructions and directives to your employees handled?

Noncontroversial Conformist: Through delegation.

Interviewer: Staff?

Noncontroversial Conformist: Yes, each ranking staff manager was delegated to issue instructions for his area of responsibility. It works out since they are aware of my feelings on the various operational considerations, and of course it was always possible for them to get in touch with me.

Interviewer: Did they bother you much?

Noncontroversial Conformist: No, not really, just a few times on items of importance. Personnel, mostly.

Interviewer: What really motivates you personally?

Noncontroversial Conformist: I'm quite interested in my work, and I want to do the best job possible for my company. I find it rewarding for the sense of accomplishment it offers.

Interviewer: Do you think only in terms of the welfare of the company or do you consider yourself too?

Noncontroversial Conformist: Well, I consider myself too I suppose. You have to, don't you? I couldn't have reached my level if I hadn't considered myself.

Interviewer: How do you consider your own interests?

Noncontroversial Conformist: By doing my best for the company mostly. I try to get along with everybody too, and some of the higher-level executives are my friends. Not that I'm implying that has anything to do with it directly.

Interviewer: You mentioned your friends. Do you think you have any people who might oppose you in any way?

Noncontroversial Conformist: I certainly hope not. No, I don't think so. I try to get along with everybody, and I don't believe there are any who "oppose me," as you put it.

Interviewer: Have you pushed through any major changes yourself in an effort to improve your operations?

Noncontroversial Conformist: No, actually there's no need to. As I mentioned, most innovations are originated by our R and D people or the procedural methods group at [headquarters city.]

Interviewer: Do you consider your firm to be objective, that is, totally interested in its own welfare?

Noncontroversial Conformist: Yes, of course. Why do you ask that?

Interviewer: Some firms aren't totally objective. Does yours always take an objective approach to operations, personnel . . .

Noncontroversial Conformist: Well, wait now, we're not perfect if that's what you mean. I don't know how to explain it. We're objective within the bounds of directing ourselves toward a common goal. We have to give and take some. How can you tell in a complex operation like this what is and isn't objective?

Interviewer: To what degree does an individual manager's interest in furthering his own interests influence the way he operates?

Noncontroversial Conformist: Appreciably, I'd say. You have to consider the effect of what you say and do, and how you approach things will affect others, especially your superiors. You can't lose sight of that. I mean you can't just go barreling straight ahead all the time. People have feelings.

Interviewer: You can't always take a direct approach?

Noncontroversial Conformist: No, certainly not. Oh, I'd say usually you can. But sometimes you have to rely on your associations with others to help you accomplish whatever it is you are trying to do. I consider this as diplomacy.

Interviewer: You often negotiate?

Noncontroversial Conformist: Certainly. Yes. I'd say this is true within any business. To operate effectively, you have to be willing to compromise. Otherwise, you would be in opposition with each other.

Interviewer: You mean your goals are not the same?

Noncontroversial Conformist: Why, yes, certainly they are. I'm getting confused. I'm merely trying to point out that when you are dealing with people you have to consider the personal factors, such as how people feel in general and about specific items. Otherwise you can't accomplish anything. Let's face it, this company like any other is composed of people working for a common cause, but they're still people, not machines.

Interviewer: Yes, I agree. How is promotability determined?

Noncontroversial Conformist: We base it on capability, the ability to do the job, considering of course the long-range necessity for developing managers for the higher-level positions. I'd say it's on a combination of ability and potential.

Interviewer: You mean the best qualified person may not be advanced if another who is considered to have more total potential is reasonably capable of the assignment?

Noncontroversial Conformist: In effect, yes, that's true. We have to consider our need for upper-level executives and bring the more able managers along as rapidly as we can.

Interviewer: Are they usually capable of performing their duties adequately?

Noncontroversial Conformist: Generally, yes. They learn rapidly for the most part. They usually have capable subordinates who can be a lot of help.

Interviewer: Run it for them?

Noncontroversial Conformist: Well, yes—no, well partly. Maybe for a short period. These are the more capable managers, and as I say, they learn rapidly. They do O.K.

Interviewer: How are they selected?

Noncontroversial Conformist: On capability and potential. These are the more capable managers as I pointed out. They've shown they can produce, get along well with people, and are the more poised and polished men.

Interviewer: In summary, the managers in your department work together diplomatically in an effort to reach common goals, which requires some compromise.

Noncontroversial Conformist: That's about it.

The Noncontroversial Conformist interviewed is an excellent example of this type of manager. He was very cordial and cooperative. The interview was conducted in a pleasant and relaxed manner. It was rather difficult to get any specific information, not that the Noncontroversial Conformist was withholding anything, but because there was little specific information to obtain.

This manager stated that he believed in leading his people rather than in driving them, but no evidence of either method was elicited in the interview. The interview did reveal that he had used a plant tour to get acquainted with his employees. As a result, he made several suggestions for improved operations, but they were inconsequential. Under the circumstances, it is understandable that his suggestions were "well received."

He next mentioned formal in-plant training programs in which he encouraged his managers to participate. When he was asked about specific instructions that he gave the men, he mentioned the meetings in which his line as well as staff employees made suggestions and the meetings in which his staff specialists made presentations and introduced "procedural modifications."

The Noncontroversial Conformist when again asked about his specific directives said he based them on studies and recommendations of his staff heads.

He often referred to interdepartmental meetings in which he coordinated his department's activities. He also mentioned peripheral staff operations for which he was responsible but to which he obviously paid little attention, or at least seldom participated in.

This management approach is typical of the *nonmanaging manager* whose organization seems to operate very well during his absence. This, however, is true of other managerial approaches in large bureaucratic organizations whose supporting staffs readily fill any void created by the absence of the ranking executive.

The Noncontroversial Conformist recognized the importance of self-interest and used friendships and his ability to get along well with people. He had no known enemies in the organization.

He viewed the unofficial or nondirect actions as cooperative effort directed toward a common goal, the welfare of the business. He did not view the degree of unofficial actions required in his company as unusual and seemed to accept it as the natural course of corporate events. He was cognizant of the personal factors and that "people have feelings" and conducted himself accordingly.

His comments on promotability indicate that sometimes the best qualified person is not promoted if higher management has selected another person who has long-range potential. Sometimes as a result, managers move so rapidly that they must be supported by their more experienced employees.[1] It's possible that the Noncontroversial Conformist interviewed readily falls in this category.

Noncontroversial Conformists at Amalgamated

The Noncontroversial Conformist interviewed was Collins, the general plant manager of Amalgamated.

Denley, a foreman, found Collins' tour of the plant somewhat amusing:

> Mr. Collins went around meeting everybody soon after he was promoted to general plant manager. He made a good impression on everyone, perhaps due in part to our being used to Hill. Mr. Collins seems to be a very nice person, and I prefer him to Hill. But it's quite a change.

Mr. Collins told us how they operated at [another plant] and asked us to start using a stick-on deal for inventory flow control. We'd used it before sometime back, but it was just more unnecessary paper work. But we said fine and started again. He made some other comments too, and the section managers followed him around taking notes so they wouldn't miss anything. It was all a bunch of piddling stuff.

Mr. Collins didn't know a thing about [the line operation] as far as I could tell. Hairgrove was explaining some of it and got it all mixed up and Mr. Collins didn't know the difference.

Collins had moved rapidly in the organization and was apparently lacking in technical knowledge. Most directives were prepared for his authorization by his supporting staff employees who were well versed in the operations. Under his *democratic* or committee leadership approach, the plant operation generally maintained the previous levels. There was a difference of opinion concerning his leadership as compared with Hill's dictatorial approach.

The comments of Parks (O-3), a section manager, are an indication of his high degree of self-interest. Parks seems to be pleased with Collins' management because of the freedom it gives.

Our plant operation is running smoothly under Collins and there is less pressure. Ayers is a good man, and I think things are better than they have been for some time. Hill was always poking around and Collins does, too, but it's different in that you don't have to be on guard with Collins.

Another section manager, Carr, (E-3), showed concern for the plant.

We seem to have lost our sense of direction somewhat. We have to have very well-defined objectives to shoot at and these are becoming somewhat vague under Collins. Our people let down some if we take the pressure off, and sometimes I'm not absolutely sure what's expected.

We are doing pretty well compared to [other plants] but I'd feel better if things were better defined. I've learned through the years that our measurements should be set high enough to make us extend ourselves. If we get complacent, a day of reckoning will come.

The "day of reckoning" did come shortly after Ayers was promoted and transferred to another plant. Ayers was replaced by Johnson, a Dictator.

Collins *suggested* that production levels be increased for a more favorable comparison with other plants and Johnson accepted this as a directive and *crashed* production to get the results which were expected. Maintenance suffered, there were personnel losses because of excessive job pressures, and the experience factor decreased.

The combination of a Noncontroversial Conformist supervisor and a dictatorial employee in this case contributed to decreased efficiency since the dictatorial insistence on results was not tempered from above.

Noncontroversial Conformists at Wildcat

Tooler, the head of the legal department, was first employed by Wildcat as a consultant, and he had been with Wildcat longer than any of the other employees. With his experience, Tooler was well acquainted with the managers and their managerial approaches.

I first met Jake and Schmidt after they had been in the Desdemona (Hogtown) operation. They had been drillers in the Ranger field prior to that and knew a lot more about drilling than they did about handling the vast amount of money they had made and were making at Desdemona. They knew they could lose all they made about as easily as they made it, as had happened to most in the adjacent Ranger field.

I was just starting my practice in those days, and I provided legal advice on their lease operations at first. Later I went on a retainer and ultimately handled the incorporation. After the corporation was formed, I spent so much of my time on Wildcat they offered me a full-time job which developed into the head of the legal department.

I was instrumental in the formative stages in the development of the business and the selection of people. I was more of a business manager than a legal counsel. I handled the administrative part, and they provided the technical knowledge—and the money, of course. I had a minor interest even then.

Most of the original employees are gone now, but some like Baker and Quafin and Tate have been around quite awhile. Quafin was in lease control before Hawkins and later was made V.P. Operations. He was quite smooth in leasing, got along well and knew the right people. He's quite personable, as you know. He was not as aggressive as Hawkins. Schmidt put him in operations when things leveled off. I think he anticipated what would happen after Jake passed on, losing control I mean, which of course did occur.

Quafin, a Noncontroversial Conformist and vice president-operations, had no delusions as to his qualifications for his position and the reason he had been advanced.

Schmidt knew, with the prevailing trends in the industry and his impending loss of control, that our operations would gradually be limited to our leasing operations and our physical facilities would eventually be eliminated. That's how I came here from leasing. I knew I'd eventually work myself out of a job in effect, since the principal part of my duties would be in selling off our physical facilities and closing down the camps.

You may consider it rather odd that the old man [Schmidt] would choose me rather than a hatchet-man type for this, but he has a real feeling for the company and for our people. I know most of our employees pretty well and it hasn't been an easy thing, but what will be will be. Of course I have the field offices under my direction now, including the field leasing activities, so I stay busy.

The situation described by Quafin is somewhat unusual in that a personable and highly respected Noncontroversial Conformist was selected for the task of disposing of facilities and the employees, many with considerable service, who were no longer required. Schmidt obviously selected Quafin so that the employees' departure would be as painless as possible. It is probable that Schmidt also recognized that Quafin would conform to Wildcat's expectations by not attempting to find alternate solutions, a valid assumption as shown by Quafin's acceptance of "what will be will be."

Schmidt gave his reasons for selecting Quafin and discussed Quafin's qualifications:

> Hell, that Quafin gets along with everybody. Did a good job in leasing as long as he had a pusher like Hawkins under him. Quafin knows everybody, not well, maybe, but he knows them and they know him. Does what you tell him to do. Trouble is, he don't do much unless he's told. He never upsets no applecarts for damn sure. That's why I put him where he is. And it's a good thing I did, the way things turned out. You got to have the right man in the right place, and Quafin belongs right where he's at.

> He sure didn't belong in Ranger. He'd have been eaten alive. They had dives all over the place. Once we had four or five killings in one day. A man had to be a man just to survive in them days.

The driller on the Ranger discovery-well was Frank Champion,* who brought in the John McCleskey in October, 1917. Mr. Champion recalled the boom days at Ranger in the following statement:

> The townspeople would complain about the lawlessness back during the boom to Mayor Hagaman who lived on his ranch east of Ranger. He'd come in to check on it, but everybody knew he was coming, and they'd clean everything up—hide the gambling equipment and liquor and start selling cokes. The girls would all be nice and selling cokes. Then Hagaman would go back to the ranch and write an article for the paper saying what a clean town Ranger was.

Schmidt's comments on Quafin who "sure didn't belong in Ranger" are indirectly supported by Mr. Champion's observations. (This is considered in further detail in the chapter on opportunism.)

---

*Mr. Champion was interviewed in his apartment at the Gholson Hotel in Ranger, Texas, on October 15, 1967. At the age of 88 he was in good health and expressed himself quite well.

Noncontroversial Conformists at Diversified

There were no Noncontroversial Conformists in management at the Diversified plant. The dictatorial operational philosophy supported by the organization and the dictatorial approach used by Hopkins precluded this classification. Noncontroversial Conformists cannot often survive in an objective corporate environment which stresses measurable results.

Those individuals who might under other corporate circumstances tend toward noncontroversial conformity must, in an environment such as at this Diversified plant, conform to the company's expectations of dynamic leadership. The failure or inability to comply limits promotability.

The headquarters organization at Diversified does have Noncontroversial Conformists as well as all other classifications. Parts of the organization are less objective than is the case study plant and are much more bureaucratic. Noncontroversial Conformists usually require a bureaucratic organization with supporting staff operations, since without the formalized structure and procedures a greater degree of personal involvement is required.

Summary

The operational philosophy of the Noncontroversial Conformist is in almost direct opposition to that of the Dictator. When asked how he directed his people, the Dictator said he established objectives, goals, and budgets. The Noncontroversial Conformist did not give a direct answer to this question since he operated in a bureaucratic organization and passed directives along, relied on his supporting staff, and established some of the objectives by meeting with his employees "so they could throw it out on the table."

The Dictator *motivated* his people with a rigid system of controls which he considered "inviolable," and by follow-up actions. He relied on discipline and "daily hammering at the individual manager" along with "a little ranting and raving." The Noncontroversial Conformist did not mention a system of controls specifically, although such systems were used in his company. His approach was based on a friendly, fairly relaxed participative approach.

It appears superficially that a Noncontroversial Conformist could not operate effectively, and yet many are quite successful managers. There are several reasons for this. An accomplished Noncontroversial Conformist is well liked, and is respected by at least most of his employees, peers, and supervisors. He relies principally on his social skills. Since he seldom takes a stand on issues, he does not create friction. Consequently, there is no reason not to like him.

Perhaps the most important consideration is that very few people recognize a Noncontroversial Conformist. Employees of companies such as Diversified which do not have this classification of manager find it difficult to understand how such managers are permitted in other organizations. Some employees of organizations which do have Noncontroversial Conformists readily recognize them, but others in the same organization are less perceptive and do not.

One manager made these comments about Noncontroversial Conformists in his company and in another company:

> We have quite a few of them here, and it seems remarkable to me that more people don't recognize them. A lot of my co-workers wouldn't know one if they were sitting next to him. As a matter of fact, some of them are.
>
> Maybe why I recognize them so easily is my previous experience with [a major oil company]. About the only people who got ahead were this type of managers who don't manage. Things run just as well when they aren't there. I can't operate that way and that's one reason I left them. Talk about conformity and don't-rock-the-boatitus, they had it.

Another manager in the same company typified those who are unable or unwilling to recognize the Noncontroversial Conformists:

> I don't understand how there can be a nonmanaging manager. I don't think there is such a thing. And I don't understand the allegations

made . . . against some of our bosses. I consider several of them to be highly qualified and effective executives and just because people like them doesn't mean there is something wrong with them. They seem to know what they're doing as far as I can tell.

You take [name], he has the qualities you expect in an executive. And I've always respected him. It seems to me [some] are trying to say just because someone is a gentleman he's a lousy manager. I don't know what they're talking about.

Some employees were remarkably reluctant to view those managers they liked or respected with total objectivity. However, in most cases the employees viewed others as individuals without regard to managerial approaches. This is understandable since almost all employees direct their attention to things other than academic analyses of their corporate environment. Those managers in companies which had Noncontroversial Conformists and did not recognize them as such were usually at the lower levels of supervision, had limited experience, or most or all of their experience was with one company. They had accepted the operational philosophy including this managerial approach as normal and proper.

The Noncontroversial Conformists as with other classifications of managers may be mild or extreme examples. These managers are often quite successful due to their ability to get at least acceptable results through their employees. And as with other classifications, the highly skilled Noncontroversial Conformist may be a much more valuable employee than those in other classifications who have lesser abilities.

The Noncontroversial Conformists outnumber both the Dictators and the Opportunists, although more Technicians and Executives were reported by industry in general. Eight percent of the major companies state that they have more Noncontroversial Conformists than any other classification. This indicates that they have a Noncontroversial Conformist or a conforming operational philosophy. When we consider the obvious inclination to consider one's managers as Executives, this degree of candor by the companies researched is significant.

Literature Cited

1. Accelerated training programs, their reported benefits and some disadvantages, are discussed by Thomas J. Murray in "The Rise of the Fast-Track Executive," *Dun's Review*, XCIX (January, 1968), p. 34.

12 : the executive

The Executive—the outstanding, truly dedicated manager whose productive motivation is company directed and whose self-interest is constructive—is often found in the top echelons of successful organizations. This manager usually has a flexible approach to fit the particular situation.

Interview with an Executive

Interviewer: How do you approach the management of your organization?

Executive: Management is a complex subject, and there's no easy answer to that. I attempt to do it fairly—considering the job requirements and the people involved.

Interviewer: You are concerned for the feelings of people?

Executive: Not exclusively. I am concerned, yes, but management entails a variety of things—only one of which is people and their feelings. I am concerned more with equitable treatment of people than feelings as such. We can't run a business based on what people want. What they want might be directly opposite to what others want anyway. People are a complicated subject.

Interviewer: You are concerned with job requirements you said.

Executive: That's the ultimate purpose of any business. Survival of the business and advancement of its purpose.

Interviewer: How do you approach your people in your efforts to insure the survival of the business?

Executive: I don't have a simple answer for that. It depends on what we are talking about and the specific circumstances. I attempt to have as much factual information available as possible so that any instructions I originate are the proper instructions. We have certain requirements we must meet, and I attempt to arrive at the most logical and effective approach to the operation of the business.

Interviewer: How do you get your factual information?

Executive: I rely on those people who are in the best position to advise me, and I analyze whatever it is we are working on myself. I want to keep abreast of things personally to the degree that is appropriate and as my time permits. I also attempt to keep in touch with the actual operations so I know what is going on.

Interviewer: How do you direct your people on what you want them to do?

Executive: We have a formalized system we use principally. I do it in writing—letters usually, or memos. This provides a record at both ends.

Interviewer: Do you tell them what to do or just suggest?

Executive: Both. I issue direct instructions on some matters and on others I suggest they consider certain factors so they have some leeway to operate effectively under whatever circumstances exist. Or sometimes a combination of both. It depends.

Interviewer: Do you permit your employees to make suggestions?

Executive: Yes, of course. Some of our ideas come up to me. After all, it's the people who actually produce who are in a position to know what's going on. Theory on paper may not always be right in actual practice. I encourage suggestions, but I don't want a lot of unnecessary criticism of our procedures. I accept any valid suggestions.

Interviewer: Do you delegate a great deal?

Executive: In certain areas I do. I have to have confidence in others. I couldn't possibly know everything or do everything myself. But I don't turn the job over to my assistants either. I know pretty well what's going on, although I'm into some matters in greater detail than others.

Interviewer: Do you use a committee approach very much?

Executive: Some. Not exclusively, certainly. I have to rely on others, and we often meet so we can arrive at the proper solution. I don't think you can rely on the committee approach on everything, though. Ultimately, someone has to reach a decision.

Interviewer: You reach the decisions?

Executive: Quite often I do. I choose to believe they are usually the decisions that an objectively functioning group of informed managers would reach.

Interviewer: You feel you are usually right?

Executive: Nobody is always right. I just hope I am most of the time.

Interviewer: How would you summarize your overall approach?

Executive: I don't know that I can. It all depends on the specific circumstances.

Interviewer: You don't have a rigid method then?

Executive: No. Effective management requires some flexibility. My approach varies with conditions. For example, if you have major problems, I think a stronger approach is required than for normal conditions.

Interviewer: You mean the right approach at the right time under the right circumstances?

Executive: In essence, yes. One approach won't always work. You have to consider to what people, too. Some people, usually the so-called workers, require a strong approach. I found that out years ago as a first-level supervisor. Others don't. It depends. Some want to be told what to do and expect it. Others produce better in a more permissive situation. By that I mean they have some initiative.

Interviewer: Do you have people who have a pronounced managerial approach in your company?

Executive: Some seem to. Perhaps most do.

Interviewer: Are they effective managers?

Executive: Some are quite good. I don't think it would be proper for me to criticize anyone specifically. I will say that some have a strong approach under any circumstances, and others may be just the opposite.

Interviewer: Some have a dictatorial approach and others are milder and tend to conform pretty well?

Executive: Yes, well, I guess that about describes it.

Interviewer: What motivates you personally?

Executive: Humm, well, I want to be able to provide adequately for my family, and at the same time I have a definite responsibility to the company. You get into the hierarchy of needs, don't you?

Interviewer: Yes. Could you be more specific?

Executive: One thing is job satisfaction, and then there's recognition, we all need that, and a sense of belonging to something worthwhile. Maybe a way to justify your existence. O.K.?

Interviewer: O.K. Do you have managers who are more interested in themselves than they are in the company?

Executive: I'm not in a position to judge that accurately, but I suppose there are some, yes. I imagine that's true of any company.

Interviewer: Some show a little opportunism?

Executive: More than a little sometimes. I don't permit that if I'm aware of it, although I'm sure there is some in my organization. It's difficult to combat.

Interviewer: How concerned do you think your company is in its own welfare?

Executive: You're talking about people, really. The management team is quite concerned generally, but not totally, I'm afraid. Like you said, we have some—what did you call it?

Interviewer: Opportunism?

Executive: Yeah, that's it. I think the company—its people—are pretty well interested in the company. We could stand some improvement I suppose.

Interviewer: Do you always take a direct approach to resolving any problems?

Executive: Not always. You must consider what others in the organization have to lose or gain from their departmental standpoint.

Interviewer: You have department rivalry?

Executive: Yes, some. It's inevitable I suppose. You can't look at everything as black or white. It's sometimes difficult to tell what really is the best thing overall. I don't have the complete answer to that. I don't think anyone does.

Interviewer: Do you have to be careful how you approach others on major items that could affect them?

Executive: You always have to be careful. Or at least consider the circumstances. People are people, you know. That includes me too. I'm easier to get along with if people use a little diplomacy.

Interviewer: You'd rather compromise than upset someone?

Executive: I didn't say that. Sometimes you have to, of course, but I don't care for it. A person should have the strength of his convictions, and it helps to have the right convictions. I compromise some if I have to, but no more than is absolutely necessary. I'm not a yes man, and I don't care for the type.

Interviewer: What would you say is your most important responsibility as far as general management goes?

Executive: I don't know. Personal integrity perhaps. Or developing my managers and teaching them. Management done properly is a teaching job to a large extent. Doing the best I know how to do.

Interviewer: You try to do your best for your company?

Executive: I try to. I could doubtlessly do more, but yes, I try to do what I can.

The Executive interviewed was aware of the importance of people to the organization but was more concerned for fair and equitable treatment than for individual feelings. We can assume he knew that all employees could not be satisfied at all times and that effective management requires decisions which sometimes affect the individuals adversely.

This Executive operated with a flexible managerial approach. He relied on others but reached decisions himself as required. He delegated as he thought appropriate but reserved the actual control. Instructions consisted of both directives and suggestions and he permitted his employees some degree of creativity.[1]

He recognized the Dictators, Noncontroversial Conformists, and Opportunists but was unwilling to express the criticism he apparently felt toward some. He was also unwilling to discuss nonconstructive self-interest.

He also recognized the lack of total objectivity in his company and the need for unofficial actions that accompany a lack of almost total objectivity. The requirement for unofficial actions is inferred from the Executive's remarks that the degree of diplomacy and thoughtfulness necessary in his company would be appropriate in any company.

Finally, the Executive felt strongly about teaching his employees or working through motivated people who in turn were taught to motivate others.

Executives at Wildcat

Both Schmidt and Tooler of Wildcat were rated as Executives with about equal self-interest and company interest. Both were part owners of the business—which usually results in constructive interest in the enterprise. This does not account fully for Schmidt's attitude toward the business, however.

Schmidt felt some antipathy toward those oilmen whose wealth resulted more from chance than from personal involvement:

> We have these old goats come up here all the time to chew the rag and look at the girls. Their daddies was mostly dry-land farmers who just happened to be sitting on a pool of oil.

> They come up here in old blue jeans and boots and talk about having to go out and earn some beans. They usually go down and take up Hawkins' time and then wander up here like I ain't got nothing better to do than listen to them. Most of them is rich, but maybe not so rich as they make out. Then they go back and crawl in a old beat-up pickup truck or a new Caddy, whichever they're driving, and go bother somebody else.

> They're character actors, that's all they are. Character actors. We put up with them 'cause we got their leases. Bunch of damn character actors.

Schmidt had lost control of Wildcat soon after his partner Jake's death because of the stock sold by Jake's many heirs. He and Tooler as well as most employees had expected that the chairman of the board, Keeton, who had gotten control, would eventually sell the interest he owned or controlled to another company.

Tooler commented on Schmidt's executive talents:

> The Old Man was always carrying on about the character actors who hung around, the ones whose land we had under lease and who came up here for lack of something better to do. I'll tell you something else, though. The Old Man was the biggest character actor of them all.

> Schmidt knew everything that went on. He didn't miss a thing . . . . He knew about all there was to know about the business. He knew as much about the legal aspects as I did. The Old Man's the one who created the company and made it what it was.

> When I got word that Keeton had sold out, I went up to the Old Man's office to tell him. Of course we had expected it quite awhile. Anyway, I went in and told him.

> He sat there and looked out the window awhile. Finally he turned to me and said, "If that Jake hadn't of been so damn prolific, this wouldn't have happened." I nodded, and then he said, "Hell, don't just sit there. We got to start us a new company."

Wildcat, as such, no longer exists.

Executives at Amalgamated

Templo, the general plant manager, was promoted and replaced by Ayers, who had previously been the department head. Most of the management team was pleased with this appointment, as was Forney:

> Ayers began to run things pretty much as he had when he was the department head. Our paper results dropped a little immediately because everybody started to take an interest in the business again. But I think they thought if they dropped too much Ayers wouldn't look good, so they pitched in and did what they could. Ayers didn't have to do anything at first but be there.

Ayers started cleaning up and after a few months we were in pretty fair shape. Production wasn't as high but expenses were down and quality was up. And I understand our net profits went up too.

Potts, a section manager, also commented on the changes under Ayers:

One of the foremen [Denley] had been doing fine under Templo, and it looked like he would make section manager before long. But then Templo got promoted and left. Denley kept right on like he was before, but that was a mistake. He got warned once about an unethical practice, and then Ayers fired him. Or had him fired. After that everybody took a real interest in running the job right. It's a shame in a way. I know it was the foreman's fault he got fired, but still if Templo had stayed he would probably have been promoted. It's hard to say who's to blame.

Under Ayers the plant operation improved, though not necessarily in all phases on paper. The general morale of the plant facility was also reportedly improved.

Executives at Diversified

The second ranking manager at Diversified was rated as an Executive with almost equal self-interest and company interest. He was described by a foreman:

Mr. Irvin is a lot more friendly than Mr. Hopkins, and he's real capable too. He doesn't push as hard as Mr. Hopkins and he seems to take more of an interest in the personnel department and things like that. I think he and Mr. Hopkins make a good team. Mr. Hopkins got the plant straightened out and Mr. Irvin helped. I think they both are top executives.

Irvin not only took an interest in industrial relations, but conducted the management-development training. He seemed to act as a buffer between the dictatorial ranking executive and the rest of the management team. He was highly respected by all the managers.

Possibly Irvin was selected for his position by headquarters management so that he would complement his immediate supervisor's dictatorial approach—and possibly to assume the duties of plant manager after the plant was running properly and Hopkins had been promoted. These are suppositions and were not verified. Such planning is reasonable, however, since the plant needed a manager such as Hopkins to redirect the plant operation. After the situation is corrected, a less dynamic approach would be appropriate.

Summary

Industry generally reports having slightly more Executives than all other classifications, with the exception of the Technicians.

The executive approach to management is the most effective since it combines the flexibility required for changing conditions[2] with a sincere interest in the business, ethical practices, and the constructive self-interest that is necessary for self-development. The Executive is concerned with the welfare of the business, the welfare of his employees, and with his own welfare.

Literature Cited

1. Guest, pp. 40-81.

2. Katz and Kahn, pp. 325-327.

13 : the corporate promotables

Who are the Corporate Promotables? Why are they promotable? Or not promotable? What qualities do the promotables possess—and the nonpromotables lack? How high in the corporate structure can they rise with what qualities?

Is promotability an accurate measurement of managerial ability? Is it based on such objective criteria as dedication, loyalty, technical knowledge, and hard work as most managers assume? Or is it only a statistical measurement of personal advancement?

What are the pitfalls to be avoided and the qualities to develop for promotability?

Throughout this book we have been concerned with the requirements for promotability within organizations. Basic to promotability is a sound balance between company interest and the motivating self-interest drives of achievement, ego, and power aspirations. Properly motivated through these self-directed drives, striving managers also need to develop the sensitivity to recognize the formal and informal expectations of the executive organization and the ability and willingness to adapt to these expectations.

For most managers, promotions serve as signs of success within the organization. And yet, many organizations seemingly ignore the potential motivational spur built into an objective appraisal program. Such firms may also overlook the importance of an objective managerial philosophy as a guide for company actions. These organizations suffer from the ravages of nonobjectivity and so do the individuals employed by them.

171

One of the more important aspects of objectivity is the mutual understanding between managers and the organization as to just what is expected of the managers. Organizations need to spend considerably less attention on attempting to motivate employees to exert more effort in their jobs and more attention on directing such effort. Much more attention must be given to developing a clearer understanding of the Expectancy Balance (EB) among management personnel. The better the understanding between the managers and the organization concerning what is expected, the better the individual can direct his efforts toward the goals of the organization and for his own benefit. And, of course, the assessment of the manager's ability will be more rational and objective.

In general, the promotable manager must have sufficient self-interest and sufficient perception and adaptability. These managers are the Corporate Promotables—the Dictators, the Opportunists, the Executives, the Noncontroversial Conformists, and to a lesser degree, the Technicians.

They have learned that promotability is based directly on corporate expectations and that those individuals who correctly perceive their roles by adapting to the organization's requirements are promotable. "The men who want to advance rapidly must pay particular attention to the expectations and standards of the men who govern their chances for promotion."[1] Most people learn from experience that it pays to adapt their behavior to environmental pressures, but if this adaptation entails a radical departure from the individual's inner motivation or self-image, it cannot be made without serious strain.[2]

The Dictators

In many organizations such as Diversified the prevailing dictatorial philosophy creates an atmosphere of acceptance and promotability for the Dictators. In companies with other operational philosophies, the Dictators are promotable, but the dictatorial approach is not predominant. Companies such as Amalgamated have Dictators even though the prevailing operational philosophy, while not clearly defined, leans more toward opportunism.

The degree of individual dictatorial methods must also be viewed in relation to the organization. What might be considered a high degree of individual dictatorialism in one company could be considered mild in a company in which the dictatorial philosophy is deeply embedded.

The Dictators are promotable in companies which have a dictatorial operational philosophy because they accurately judge the role expectancies of the organization.[3] They are also promotable in companies with less than total objectivity which do not have a dictatorial operational philosophy. In these companies they display the image of hard-driving, forceful managers who are company oriented and who can produce the expected results. That Dictators are seldom highly successful in producing results that are in the best interest of the company and that such managers are self-oriented rather than company oriented are conditions apparently unrecognized by those higher-level managers who provide their high degree of promotability.

Research has shown that the managers and other employees who work for these authoritarians are more likely to have unfavorable attitudes toward their job and the organization than are members of groups led by more considerate leaders. Further, employees working for such Dictators are more likely to take out their frustrations through excessive waste and scrap loss, higher rates of turnover and absenteeism, less concern with costs, and a larger number of grievances that go to arbitration. These grievances frequently lead to a greater frequency of slow-downs, work stoppages, and similar difficulties.[4]

The Opportunists

Some companies do not have Opportunists because a high degree of corporate objectivity precludes opportunism. Those who in less objective companies would tend toward opportunism must, in their own self-interest, suppress these tendencies and develop a different approach in objective organizations. Because Opportunists are self-oriented, they normally adapt to the corporate expectations which in objective companies are not directed toward opportunism. Consequently, individuals with opportunistic tendencies are not allowed to become opportunistic in objective organizations.

Such opportunistic managers may be Dictators in companies in which this philosophy prevails, or even if the company does not have a dictatorial management philosophy. They may be Noncontroversial Conformists in companies which reward this approach with promotability. Some may be Executives.

Opportunists are promotable because their actions are self-oriented and are designed to produce promotability rather than to produce for the company. These individuals adapt to their company's expectations and usually attempt to excel in producing paper results. Since they are often unconcerned with the ethics of their methods, the possibility of obtaining recognition is broadened—providing additional potential promotability.

Opportunists are also promotable because of the inability or unwillingness of their supervisors to recognize opportunism. If the supervisors are unable to recognize blatant opportunism, they are lacking in perception. If, however, they are unwilling to recognize opportunism, they are displaying their own opportunism. Opportunism in the lower levels of the organization is not only an indication of nonobjectivity but is an indication of at least some opportunism at the upper level of management.

The Noncontroversial Conformists

The Noncontroversial Conformists are promotable in organizations with less than almost total objectivity, often highly promotable. They are especially promotable in organizations which operate with a conforming operational philosophy. They have limited promotability in highly objective organizations and in organizations with a dictatorial climate.

These chameleons who are so classified because of their planned conformity adapt to the corporate expectations. In companies which do not tolerate this classification, these conforming managers normally adapt to the organization's

requirements and become promotable in some acceptable classification. Those individuals whose personalities place them in the
Noncontroversial Conformist classification and who are unable or
unwilling to adapt to another classification have limited promotability in objective companies.

Many individuals who fall in this classification do so as a result
of their own personal adjustment to social relationships. They
must have the acceptance of others. This requires them to avoid
controversial issues and strong personal convictions. Their *normal*
approach to interpersonal relationships precludes conflict and so
they are accepted. It is this basic need for acceptance which
produces the *pure* Noncontroversial Conformist.

Other individuals develop this approach as a planned method
of meeting company expectations. These are usually the *fence
riders* who may or may not have personal warmth in interpersonal
relationships. The most successful Noncontroversial Conformists
are those who fit in this classification naturally. These managers
often have personal warmth which they shower on any other
individual regardless of the individual's own acceptability to
others. No person is rejected by the Noncontroversial Conformist,
and therefore he is also accepted by all others. The depth of a
Noncontroversial Conformist's relationship with other individuals
is another matter.

Noncontroversial Conformists are also promotable because of
the almost complete inability of many people to recognize them
for what they really are.

The Technicians

The Technicians have limited promotability in almost any
organization. These workers are often viewed as the solid
foundation on which the organization is built. Those few
Technicians who are promotable to the third level of large
bureaucratic organizations are normally the more highly skilled
individuals and they often have college educations.

Technicians who are not promotable don't recognize that hard
work, loyalty, and company interest are not sufficient for
promotability. They often lack the perception or sensitivity to

recognize what their company's expectations for promotability actually are. They also often lack the self-interest that is required to develop themselves for promotability. Some who do recognize that self-interest is required are totally incapable of directing themselves toward constructive self-interest. These normally find hard work—or at least work—loyalty, and company interest the path of least resistance.

It is in the Technician classification that the greatest degree of personal tragedy is experienced. The Dictators, Opportunists, and Noncontroversial Conformists have found a method of adjusting to the complex world of business and to their corporate environment, even if it is not necessarily the best adjustment. Many of the Technicians, especially the highly skilled ones, have not adjusted—with resultant limited promotability. Those who are basically capable and ambitious are frustrated and confused individuals who have been rewarded for their efforts and loyalty with nonpromotability. Few Technicians can understand what has caused the limited success of their careers.

The Executive

The Executives are promotable in any company and are highly promotable in most. However, they are not as promotable as Dictators in companies which have a dictatorial operational philosophy since they do not fit the required image. They may not be as promotable as Opportunists in some nonobjective companies because their constructive company interest may limit their promotability. In addition, Executives may not be as promotable as Noncontroversial Conformists in organizations which have an overall philosophy of conformity. In these companies, the Executives are too action oriented.

There can be little doubt that managerial behavior does affect the productivity, attitudes, and satisfactions of the members of the organization, although we have seen that any style of leadership—Dictatorial, Opportunist, Noncontroversial Conformist, Executive—may be either successful or unsuccessful, depending on the organization. Negative attitudes and satisfactions can hurt management in the most sensitive part of its anatomy— the pocketbook.

In objective companies, though, the Executive seems to foster better attitudes and satisfactions in his people than do other types of managers. The reasons are simple: (1) he tends to be more participative; (2) he is considerate of his employee's needs; (3) he is adept at solving group problems; (4) he *goes to bat* for his people; and (5) he seldom relies on punitive rewards.

Table 13-1

Amalgamated Electronics, Inc.,

Actual Balance by Classifications

Actual Balance	Technicians	Dictators	Executives	Opportunists	Noncontroversial Conformists
1	100%	—%	—%	—%	—%
2	71	6	7	8	8
3	7	17	22	24	30
4	—	45	6	41	8

Actual Balance and Classification

The relation between a manager's Actual Balance and his classification is shown in Table 13-1. This gives the results of an analysis of the managers at Amalgamated Electronics and shows the percentage in each classification for the four levels of self-company interest. Amalgamated is used in this and subsequent tables because it is representative of industry in general.

The 1's with almost total company interest were, without exception, Technicians. The 2's with more company interest than self-interest were mostly Technicians with a few in each of the other classifications. The Technicians were generally at the first two levels of supervision where companies expect more company interest than self-interest. Because of this expectation, many managers at the first two levels only give some indication of their *true* classification. We can assume that some managers appearing as Technicians at the lower levels will readily fit other classifications after promotion to the upper levels of the organization.

The managers with almost equal self-interest and company interest, the 3's, fell fairly evenly in all classifications except that of the Technicians. Those with almost total self-interest were fairly evenly divided between Dictators and Opportunists, with a few Executives and Noncontroversial Conformists rated high enough in self-interest to qualify as 4's.

Table 13-1 should be accepted only as an approximation because the rapid movement in a growth company such as Amalgamated can quickly alter the percentages. The trends remain the same, however.

Classification and Potential Promotability

Table 13-2 shows the relationship of classifications to potential promotability as determined by present levels, known planned promotions, and anticipated future promotions.

The average Actual Balance for each classification is the simple arithmetic average for all those in each classification. The average Actual Balance for the Technicians is only 1.61 compared with 3.86 for the Opportunists.

The average probable levels attainable for each classification are also arithmetic averages for each classification. In an organization with six levels of supervision, the Executives' average was highest at 4.07, indicating that although some Executives potentially would reach the fifth or sixth level some would not reach the fourth level.

The promotable Technicians are predominantly 2's on the Actual Balance scale. The other classifications are, of course, almost entirely 3's and 4's. The most significant comparison shown in Table 13-2 is the variance between the potential promotability of the average Technician and other types of managers. The slight difference between the others is not significant. As stated previously, the fairly rapid rate of promotions in this company can alter the comparative figures although the trends are constant.

Table 13-2

Amalgamated Electronics, Inc.,
Promotability of Classifications

	Average Actual Balance	Average Probable Levels Attainable
Technicians	1.61	1.72
Dictators	3.78	3.94
Executives	3.11	4.07
Opportunists	3.86	3.92
Noncontroversial Conformists	3.23	3.97

The percentage of managers in each classification is not shown because it varies between companies. There are usually more Technicians than there are other types because of the larger number of management people at the first and second levels than at the higher levels. Large bureaucratic companies with large operational staffs have comparatively more Technicians than do some smaller companies.

In Amalgamated the Noncontroversial Conformists outnumbered the other three classifications slightly, but this is not true in all companies since some have few, if any, because of their corporate philosophy. Industry in general seems to have more

Technicians than the other types. The other classifications are relatively equal in numbers.

The major companies, such as General Dynamics, The Prudential Insurance Company of America, The Standard Oil Company of Indiana, and many others when measured as a group, consider their management teams to have more Technicians, followed by Executives, Noncontroversial Conformists, and Opportunists—with Dictators fewest in number.

At Amalgamated the average age of 1's (with almost total company interest) was comparable to the age of the 3's and 4's rather than to that of the 2's which was considerably lower. This indicates the upward movement of the 2's with an increase in self-interest to 3's and 4's. The 3's and 4's of course were principally at the third and higher levels, were older, and had longer years of service.

Those who advanced most rapidly were college graduates who were in or had been in accelerated training programs; next were college graduates not in such programs. However, some noncollege men were highly promotable in all companies tested.

Actual Balance and Promotability

The promotable managers are promotable principally as a result of their balance between self-interest and company interest as shown in Table 13-3. Various levels of management have been weighted to the same numerical base so that percentages can be shown for comparison. With the pyramid structure of any company, of course, there are many more employees at the first (lowest) level of supervision than at the higher levels. In this case the upper levels have been included in the fifth level to provide a broader base.

The figures in Table 13-3 show that all except 8 percent of the individuals measured as 1's having almost total company interest are at the first level of supervision, and none are above the second level. A similar situation existed in all large companies researched, which indicates that those with very limited self-interest do not develop themselves for promotability.

Those rating as 2's on the Actual Balance scale were promotable to the second level with limited promotability above that. Most 2's at the third level were operational staff people.

Those with almost a balance between self-interest and company interest (3's) were almost equally divided at the third through fifth levels, as were the self-oriented 4's. There were a few 3's at the second level, however.

The minor variations between 3's and 4's at and above the third level are insignificant and may be attributed to the more

Table 13-3

Amalgamated Electronics, Inc.,
Promotability by Actual Balances

Actual	Levels of Supervision				
Balance	1	2	3	4	5
1	92%	8%	—%	—%	—%
2	45	49	6	—	—
3	—	4	31	33	32
4	—	—	32	37	31

limited number of managers available for testing at the higher levels of the pyramid.

Promotability in highly objective organizations is a fairly accurate measurement of management ability, within the limits of human judgment. However, promotability in companies with less than almost total corporate objectivity is a statistical measurement of personal advancement. In these companies, promotability is also a measurement of the manager's ability to play the correct role.

Promotability is of primary concern to the individual and therefore is quite personal. It becomes considerably impersonal when viewed by the top executive or when any manager considers the promotability of his employees or supervisors. It is the impersonal or total promotability factors which are the principal concern of the organization.

The promotability of the individual managers as related to the classifications of promotables constitutes the organization's promotability philosophy. This total promotability philosophy is the prime consideration in any organization since this is what determines who runs the company and how it is run.

The ultimate purpose in considering promotability is to make it possible to achieve a higher degree of corporate objectivity.

Literature Cited

1. William R. Dill, Thomas L. Hilton, and Walter R. Reitman, "How Aspiring Managers Promote Their Own Careers," in *Readings in Human Relations,* 2nd ed., eds. Keith Davis and William G. Scott (New York: McGraw-Hill Book Company, 1964), p. 258.

2. Paul Pigor and Charles A. Myers, *Personnel Administration,* 5th ed. (New York: McGraw-Hill Book Company, 1965), p. 109.

3. Dill, Hilton, and Reitman, *The New Managers,* p. 240.

4. Likert, *New Patterns of Management,* pp. 58-60.

14 : the corporate crisis

Management is facing an increasing challenge from a changing environment. With the knowledge explosion and the technological advances in industry, a highly efficient operation is necessary for any business to meet competition. Accordingly, a high level of corporate objectivity is becoming increasingly more important to the continued success of any organization.

In the preceding chapters we have discussed the effects of the lack of corporate and individual objectivity. Through analysis of several companies and from the insights provided by managers at all levels of management, we have indicated the adverse results of nonobjectivity to show that corrective action is necessary and to suggest methods of correction.

Managerial behavior, whether objective or nonobjective, is based upon some form of management theory. Consciously or subconsciously, managers rely on generally accepted values and beliefs concerning successful modes of action. These beliefs or theories have considerable influence on management thought and practice. An understanding of these general theories is necessary for managers to place their philosophies of management in perspective. These basic management theories may be generalized as: the Mechanistic Doctrine, the Humanistic Doctrine, and the Modernistic Doctrine.[1]

The Mechanistic Doctrine

The Mechanistic Doctrine concentrates on the anatomy of the organization and can be traced to the philosophy of Frederick W. Taylor at the turn of the century. This Mechanistic Doctrine emphasizes techniques of management, the structure of the organization, and centralized authority in a highly regimented operation. Application of this doctrine depends largely on the use of power and authority in the organization. The Mechanistic Doctrine was developed as a direct result of the Industrial Revolution which emphasized productivity with little or no concern for the human element. The foundation of management science and management as a profession was based on this early philosophy.

Although the attitude inherent in the Mechanistic or Classical Doctrine toward personnel is considered somewhat archaic, a modern form is still in use. It is not recognized by the organizations or individual managers as such, but the dictatorial operational philosophy is based on the Mechanistic Doctrine. Modern organizations often take great pride in their progressive approach to management, yet many of these have an authoritarian philosophy or dictatorial managers who have great influence on the organization.

It is obvious that many similarities exist between the modern dictatorial philosophy and the Mechanistic approach. Both are concerned with production and emphasis on results with little consideration given to the human element. Control is centralized at the top in companies where Dictators exercise extreme authority. Initiative is discouraged and managers execute directives rather than manage. Management is largely nonparticipative.

The Mechanistic Doctrine has been supported by the Protestant Ethic. That employees have accepted this doctrine is due not only to their inability to avoid it totally, but to the Protestant Ethic which accepts hard work, often for the sake of hard work, as a prerequisite to success. The Technician in this respect supports the Mechanistic Doctrine or dictatorial philosophy with his acceptance of its principles. The relationship between the Protestant Ethic and this doctrine seriously weakens the Protestant Ethic as the sole means of promotability in today's businesses.

Douglas McGregor in *The Human Side of Enterprise* criticizes the Mechanistic Doctrine and describes it as Theory X. According to Theory X, the conventional managerial philosophy is based on the assumption that: (1) people must be controlled by the organization and the organization must modify their behavior to fit the needs of the productive enterprise; (2) people must be directed since their natural inclination is to be passive or even resistant to the organization. McGregor also views the Mechanistic Doctrine as assuming that people are inherently self-centered, lacking in ambition, gullible, and not very bright. His solution is offered as Theory Y (discussed with the Modernistic Doctrine).

In modern management these accusations, while basically sound, seem overly critical. Certainly no skilled manager views employees as completely devoid of ambition or intelligence. Yet the continued reliance on the dictatorial operational philosophy in many companies supports McGregor's contention that Theory X has not as yet been generally supplanted by modern philosophies.

The Mechanistic Doctrine was not totally acceptable to employees. Because there was little or no emphasis on the human element, the employees were often apathetic to management's objectives. In defense of the organization, management became aware of the need for a reevaluation of management techniques. During the 1920's, studies and experiments indicated that production could be increased when human relations were considered. The pioneering studies made by Mayo at the Hawthorne Plant of Western Electric, manufacturing arm of the Bell Telephone System, contributed to the knowledge and understanding of human relations.[2] The studies were originally designed to determine the effects of physical working conditions, but accidentally the benefits of individual participation in group activities with the resultant ego satisfaction were recognized.

The Humanistic Doctrine

The combination of union activities, management studies of the human element, and governmental influence led to the Humanistic or Neoclassical Doctrine. This doctrine actually began with the Mayo studies in the late 1920's but was not developed and accepted by industry in general until the post-World War II period.

The Humanistic Doctrine compensated for some of the deficiencies of the Mechanistic Doctrine in that the behavioral sciences were introduced into the theory of organization. The Humanistic Doctrine related the informal organization and unofficial actions to the formal organization.

The major contributions of this doctrine were in the fields of leadership, motivation, and employee participation. Emphasized were group dynamics, social systems, and human-relations training.

The contributions made by the human-relations approach were often overshadowed by the excesses practiced in industry. For example, many companies adopted the Humanistic approach in compensating for the excesses of the Mechanistic Doctrine. Many of them suddenly discovered that they had overcompensated in attempting to "make people happy." This approach was often reevaluated and modified considerably. Some overcompensation may have been inevitable, however, if the inequities of the Mechanistic Doctrine were to be effectively corrected.

The Humanistic approach was a necessary and valuable management advance in the evolution of management thought, but the Humanistic Doctrine was not totally successful because of the inability to integrate it completely with the economic necessity for production.

The Modernistic Doctrine

The Modernistic Doctrine had its inception with the recognition of the necessity to integrate the Humanistic Doctrine with the Mechanistic Doctrine. The Modernistic Doctrine attempts to modify these two doctrines to compensate for their errors. For example, modern management practice advocates such structural arrangements as profit centers, project management, and the use of task forces as opposed to the Mechanistic centralized control. While these techniques are basically structural, they are also humanistic in that they provide for the participation and training of lower-level managers in decision-making with resultant ego satisfaction and inner motivation.

McGregor's Theory Y is the antithesis of Theory X and is suggested by McGregor as offering more valid assumptions. It states that people are not naturally passive or resistant to the organization and are capable of objective self-control and inner motivation. The responsibility of the organization is to provide an environment conducive to people's achieving their own goals by directing their energies toward the organization's goals.

Gellerman notes that a difficulty with Theory Y is that "there is no simple formula whereby it can be applied."[3] He wryly observes also that the lack of a simple formula may be a blessing in disguise in view of our less than desirable experience with human-relations fads.

This brief look at prevailing management doctrines should impress upon managers the influence these theories have on current practices. Attempts to apply the theories or philosophies in the past have not been totally successful. The theories presented in this book build upon the theories of the past to provide a foundation for effective management practices.

The Challenge of the Future

In our discussions with managers at all levels of organizations it was apparent that while many were well informed, most were not completely conversant with management theory and principles. Of those who were at least reasonably knowledgeable, few applied their knowledge in management practice to the degree it was possible. We recognize that many managers and their companies are quite successful. The full utilization of their total capabilities, however, would increase the success of these managers and their organizations.

The lack of an analytical approach to the management function can be attributed to the daily pressures experienced by managers and the requirement for expediency in normal operations. There is also a tendency for managers to conform to existing philosophies and methods since innovation requires creativity, and creativity in any form may be subject to criticism. It is often safer for managers in organizations with less than complete objectivity to accept existing philosophies and to adapt rather than to innovate.

The creation of an objective corporate environment requires a corporate philosophy of acceptance of change and innovation and requires the effective use of available management knowledge. The most important goal of any organization is its self-perpetuation, that is, its continued existence as an organization. This requires flexibility and adaptability by the organization and its management team to survive in a technological, sociological, legal and political environment. Management must prepare now to meet the challenge of the future.

In this book we have presented organization theory in nontechnical terms to provide instruction, guidance, and insights into the complexities of organizations and to provide a theoretical foundation for the objective management of organizations.

Literature Cited

1. The doctrines presented here generally follow the discussion of these theories by William G. Scott in "Organization Theory: An Overview and An Appraisal," *Journal of the Academy of Management*, IV, 1 (April, 1961), 7-26.

2. Elton Mayo, *The Social Problems of an Industrial Civilization* (Boston: Harvard Business School, 1945); also see F.J. Roethlisberger and W.J. Dickson, *Management and the Worker* (Cambridge: Harvard University Press, 1939).

3. Saul W. Gellerman, *The Management of Human Relations* (New York: Holt, Rinehart and Winston, 1966), p. 51.

appendix one

Predicting managerial success has been an elusive goal of many organizations as they attempt to assess managerial potential. Some progressive companies, however, have been successful in developing objective methods of appraising the potential of their managers. The following articles by Charles P. Sparks and Douglas W. Bray describe the successful programs developed at Humble and AT&T.

Identify Management Potential Early *

Charles P. Sparks
Coordinator of Personnel Research
Humble Oil & Refining Co.

There is a shortage of high-caliber management talent. To illustrate this point, one need only look at the impact an individual manager can have on productivity and profitability of a work unit. For example, one research group swapped good managers to poor work units and poor managers to good work units and awaited results. When the tallies were in, the good managers had improved the poor work units much more than the poor managers had handicapped the good work units.

Another factor responsible for interest in early identification and development is the increasing complexity of business and industry. As increasing education is more desirable, men enter the work force at later and later ages. This means less time for service as a manager, particularly if the man is expected to move step by

---

*Presented at the Gulf Coast Regional Meeting of the National Petroleum Refiners Association, Beaumont, Texas. *(Hydrocarbon Processing* [April, 1967], pp. 209-211.)

step along the traditional route of experience. To this is added the fact that demands for professional-technical excellence have also increased—so have the rewards. Fine careers are possible without going into management. This has still further diminished the amount of quality personnel from which to select and develop managers.

This increasing use of the professional-technical specialist has yet another impact. A man can spend several years and receive several promotions without ever having to demonstrate his ability in decision making, delegation, coordination, relations, etc.

Still another factor is the professionalization of management. With this has come a belief that certain principles, practices and attitudes can be taught, that they do not necessarily come from experience. In fact, without guidance, ten years of experience may well be one year of experience ten times.

All business and industries today have a mandatory retirement age. Fine, though aging, managers are not permitted to stay. The Justices of the United States Supreme Court are 81, 76, 69, 68, 61, 57, 52 and 50. Five would have certainly been retired from industry. (We will not discuss here the question of whether or not they should have been retired from Court.) The list of contributing factors would be expanded even further but these should highlight the problem.

Finding Managerial Potential Early

How early can management potential be identified? After experience on the first supervisory job? Five years after employment? At the time of employment? At graduation from high school? At graduation from grammar school? At the end of kindergarten? At age two? At birth?

Some skeptics have said "Never." The president of one of our largest corporations has said, "We always know when a man has reached his ceiling. It is when we have promoted him one notch above it."

As a researcher I would say that at birth we can predict managerial potential with much better than chance expectancy. To illustrate, let us assume that 1 of 1,000 male babies can be expected to reach a managerial position which pays $25,000 per year or more. A qualified researcher could easily select 100 from the 1,000 and bet you that he had included the one at much less than the one to ten which chance would dictate.

At each additional stage of the game—kindergarten, eighth grade, high school, college, first job, etc., he could increase his accuracy and bet with greater assurance. But he would not be let off this easily. As time went on, obvious impossibles would be eliminated on the basis of general experience and judgment. Eliminated would be the high school drop out, perhaps wrongly; the non-conformist, perhaps wrongly. When a small group of essentially alike persons had been identified the researcher would be asked, "Which of these are the best bets for advancement to managerial positions?" At this stage the researcher is being asked, "Can you see something in these people that I can't see and is it related to future managerial success?"

Jersey Standard's Experience

About 1955, Humble's parent company asked the above question. The result was a five-year research project to determine the degree of confidence which could be placed on the YES answer which the researchers were sure would be forthcoming. The same question must have been asked about the same time in American Telephone & Telegraph and in General Electric. Each of these firms also embarked upon a major research project aimed at identification of characteristics of employes who were expected to provide the next generation of managers.

Let us look first at the Jersey Standard research. Very superficially and obscuring the expenditure of much blood, sweat, tears and money, the following was accomplished:

1. 443 managers, all successful but some more so than others, completed some 14 hours of testing, questionnaire completion and interviewing.
2. A criterion of relative success was constructed, consisting of salary treatment, promotional history and managerial effectiveness when compared with peers.

3. Abilities, backgrounds, personal characteristics, self perceptions, etc., were compared with the indices of relative success
to isolate the pertinent factors.
4. Mathematical formulations were developed to combine
pertinent factors so as to predict the managerial success
indices.

Was it successful? How much confidence could be placed in
the YES? To the statistically sophisticated, "The validity coefficients were in the seventies." To the unsophisticated, "Suppose a
situation had developed where approximately 5 percent of the 443
were needed, where these 5 percent should be among our best and
where NO information was available except scores on the measured factors." If the test had been used to select 5 percent, 25 of
26 would have been among the most successful, one of 26 among
the moderately successful and none would have been among the
less successful performers.

At the other end of the scale, "Suppose a situation had developed in which elimination of approximately 5 percent of the 433
was desirable and where no information was available except
scores on the measured factors." Under these conditions 19 of 21
eliminees would have been among the less successful performers,
two would have been the moderately successful and none would
have been among the more successful performers.

AT&T's Experience

One of the crosses a researcher in industry must bear is the
probability that his compatriots will not publish their research in a
manner comparable to that of the university or foundation researcher. As a result, what I can tell you about the American
Telephone & Telegraph, General Electric and other researches
comes primarily from joint participation with men of their organizations in meetings such as this and a few published papers of a
non-technical nature.

Let us look first at the AT&T work. First, let us contrast it
with the Jersey Standard activity. AT&T brought men together in

groups of 12 in an assessment center. There they were tested, interviewed, observed in group activity situations for 3½ days by a team of assessors which contained both psychologists and line managers.

The techniques used included a 2-hour interview, an in-basket test, a manufacturing problem (business game), a leaderless group discussion, projective tests, standardized paper-and-pencil tests and questionnaires, a personal history questionnarie, a short auto-biographical essay and a self-description Q-sort.

The end product was a series of ratings on 25 characteristics of the individual assessed. From this, certain predictions were made concerning the likelihood of his staying with the Bell System and the probability of his attaining middle management status. This, of course, places a high premium on the competence of the assessors.

In contrast, the Jersey Standard work combined statistically a huge number of bits and pieces of information to arrive at numerical indices which could be used to compare a man with appropriate norms. The AT&T research was longitudinal. By this I mean that the effectiveness of the assessment center technique was to be measured by periodic follow-up of the men assessed to find out what happened to them. These happenings were then related to data collected in the assessment. This follow-up activity is still going on.

The Jersey Standard research was concurrent and cross-sectional. By this I mean that the validity of the results was measured by the accuracy with which men could be classified on the criterion index. The assumption was then made that men who tested like the most successful existing managers were more likely to have later success than men who did not score in this fashion.

Was the AT&T program successful? I can't show you a table of results. I can say that shortly after the first follow-up data were accumulated, AT&T developed operational assessment centers similar to the research assessment center. The new reports were made available to appropriate line managers for their use in making personnel decisions involving promotions, training, staffing, etc. The program continues to grow.

GE's Experience

General Electric began research with 1,300 engineers. They have now followed this steadily dwindling group for over 10 years and have issued five research reports on their findings. They tested the men, secured certain background and biographical data and, in addition, put each through an intensive interview by a trained psychologist. The psychologist rated each man on these factors: experience, theoretical ability, practical-technical know-how, creative ability, identification with superiors, self-confidence, manner and appearance, poise and personality.

GE's five reports deal with

1. What are the general characteristics of GE engineers?
2. Who leaves during the early years?
3. What factors are associated with salary treatment?
4. Who gets promoted?
5. What are some of the experiences, attitudes and beliefs of these engineers as they have pursued their careers with GE?

I find the research on salary treatment to be one of the most interesting. Many researchers have demonstrated that salary is one of the best yardsticks of success as long as we do not try to cross occupational lines. GE found different characteristics across four main groups—those who had high initial salaries compared with their peers and who retained their high position, those who had low initial salary position but who moved into the high position group, those with high initial position who slipped to low and those who started low and remained low. There are many implications of these data, particularly when they are compared with the characteristics of those who leave and those who get promoted.

Sears, Roebuck Study

One of the longest continuous programs involving the use of tests as an aid in identification of management potential is that of

Sears, Roebuck. Some aspects go back at least 30 years. Here is an unusual kind of study aimed at measuring its effectiveness. The usual form of measurement is to compare the predictor data with some kind of evidence of what management thinks or has thought of the man about whom the prediction is made—ratings, rankings, salary treatment, promotion history, etc.

Sears compared the executive test scores of 48 store managers with what the employes thought as measured by surveys of the employes of the 48 stores. Correlations between executive test scores and morale scores are as follows:

Effectiveness of Administration	.77
Technical Competence of Supervision	.74
Adequacy of Communication	.59
Friendliness of Fellow Employes	.37
Supervisor-Employe Relations	.68
Confidence in Management	.59
Job Security	.40
Status and Recognition	.69
Identification with the Company	.51
Opportunity for Growth & Advancement	.37
Employe Benefits	.54
Pay	.30
Working Conditions	.36
Job Demands	.00
Over-all Morale Score	.47

The data collected from these and other studies should convince even the most skeptic individuals that identification of management potential is possible, and with a high degree of accuracy. Whether it should be done and the implications of making such data available are subjects which are not easily attacked by research methods. It will be covered here only by saying that Humble *has* decided to use the data.

Uses for Data Collected

Seven valid uses are seen:
1. Uncover promising men earlier
2. Confirm judgments; act with greater assurance
3. Assist choice for tryout as supervisors
4. Encourage early action on unpromising men
5. Provide objective base-line measurement across groups
6. Help analyze recruiting efforts
7. Develop more accurate potential estimates

More experience is needed and more research. Perhaps articles such as this will stimulate additional companies.

Locating Tomorrow's Managers Through Assessment Centers *

Dr. Douglas W. Bray
Assistant Vice President
New York Telephone Company

Over the past 13 years I have had the unusual opportunity of spending the bulk of my time on management selection and development. Since 1956 I have been the director of the Bell System Management Progress Study, a very intensive research into the development of young managers. As a by-product of that study, the assessment-center method of selecting managers has been applied to over 45,000 candidates for various levels of management. We have learned much about such candidates and their later success. More recently, in my current assignment as Assistant Vice President of the New York Telephone Company, one of my responsibilities is to keep *the book* on ready-now and promising candidates for management jobs up to, but not including, the top officer level. Today I would like to share with

---

*Given before the Spring Conference of the Industrial Relations Management Association under the direction of the University of British Columbia, Vancouver, Canada, February, 1969.

you some of the thoughts to which these opportunities to observe have led me.

There is one thing of which we can be sure. An organization will always find someone to fill each management spot, at least until it goes out of business. Vacancies have to be filled, either by moving up the best man available, even though in some instances he may not be chosen with much enthusiasm, or by direct hiring, which also has its risks. When we talk about "locating tomorrow's managers," we are not of course concerned with finding enough warm bodies to fill boxes on the organization chart, but with striving to guarantee that every future manager is highly capable in his assignment.

Finding Managers From Within

To simplify the discussion, I would like to start by ignoring the possibility of hiring directly into middle and upper management and concentrate on the organization which, with rare exceptions, finds its managers from within. Where this is the case, and it is in many instances, including the Bell System, it is of the utmost importance that barriers be erected to prevent any but those with good management potential from becoming part of that pool of employees from which the middle and upper managers of the future will be selected. This means that those employed from the colleges as management trainees and those elevated to lowest-level management from nonmanagement must be very carefully screened.

The reason for this stress on initial selection is that once there is mediocrity in the management pool some of it, usually too much of it, will find its way upward. Ordinary appraisal processes are just not reliable enough. Weak managerial abilities are often overlooked in men who have technical knowledge, but an organization cannot afford to be anything less than stringent in guarding the lowest managerial gates. If intake is of high quality, later mistakes in selection will not have as serious consequences as they might have otherwise.

A significant percentage of Bell System management, even at the higher levels, still comes from those who start with the business as vocational employees and work their way up into management. Several thousand of this so-called non-college group are promoted into first-level management every year and thus form a very large pool of employees, many of whom will rise still further in the management hierarchy.

Accurate appraisal of a vocational employee's management abilities is particularly difficult. They are usually *visible* to only one of many supervisors. To all the usual difficulties of appraisal is added the fact that production jobs do not reveal much about managerial ability. The man who gets promoted tends to be one who does his craft work well, has been around a number of years, and who doesn't give his boss any trouble. Higher management has often been dissatisfied with the selections being made but has lacked the tools to do much about it.

The Management Progress Study

In starting the Management Progress Study in 1956, we needed to establish a base line for the future longitudinal study of our subjects during their early years in management. We wanted to know as much as possible about their abilities, motivation, personality, and management potential. To secure such measurements, we put together a three-and-a-half-day assessment process which handled twelve men at a time and required a staff of nine. Shortly after our initial use of the center as a research instrument, the Plant Department of the Michigan Bell Telephone Company became interested in a trial application of the method for selecting foremen.

Some changes were made in the original research assessment center because the operational center would be staffed by nonprofessionals. Thus devices such as projective personality tests could not be used. The first center was, of course, under scrutiny by management since it was a radical and expensive innovation. Since that time, the fall of 1958, assessment has continued in the Michigan company and spread to 13 other Bell System telephone companies. There are now over 60 assessment centers testing up to 10,000 management candidates a year.

Assessing the Candidates

The Typical Bell System assessment center processes 12 candidates a week. The candidates themselves spend two to three days at the center (depending on the particular center in question). The staff uses the rest of the week for writing reports and holding evaluation conferences. While at the center, the candidate undergoes an intensive interview, a few paper-and-pencil tests of mental ability and knowledge, and several less usual evaluation tests. One of these is a half-day administrative exercise, known as the In-Basket, simulating the paper work of a management job. Another lengthy exercise is a miniature business game in which six candidates participate. The other group problem, also for six, is a leaderless group discussion preceded by formal presentations by the members of the group.

The staff evaluation conference considers each candidate separately. The reports prepared by the staff members on the candidate's performance in each exercise are read so that all members of the assessment staff gain a complete picture of the man's behavior at the assessment center. The candidate is then rated on approximately 20 characteristics relevant to success in management, such as skill in planning and organizing, decision-making ability, leadership skills, flexibility, breadth, and so forth. After the rating process is completed, the staff then discusses the candidate's potential for promotion and assigns him to one of four categories: more than acceptable, acceptable, questionable, and unacceptable. During the following week, the assessment-center director writes a descriptive report on each candidate outlining and documenting his strengths and weaknesses as seen at the center.

Assessment results are fed back to the candidate himself and to line management. Each assessee is given the option of a personal feedback and experience indicates that approximately 85 percent of the subjects elect to receive a report of their performance. This usually takes the shape of a private session with a member of the assessment staff.

The report to the line organization has taken several forms. Some centers have invited line managers to audit the staff evaluation conference. Tape recordings of the conferences have been used in some instances. In other instances the director's descriptive report has been sent to line management and supplemented by later telephone conversations where needed. Reports are sometimes directed to the candidate's immediate supervisor, but are more often fed into the line organization at a somewhat higher level.

Rejection by the assessment center does not mean that the candidate is absolutely barred from promotion. Local management is expected to make a careful comparison between the description of the man provided by the assessment process and the man's performance on his present job. Where there are discrepancies, it is management's responsibility to determine whether appraisal of the man's potential as deduced from his job performance has been off base or whether the assessment center has gained a faulty impression of the man. If the evidence is convincing enough, the assessment decision can be overridden, but it cannot be lightly ignored. That it is not is indicated by the fact that although one-third of assessment candidates are deemed unacceptable, only five percent of this group has been promoted.

The Assessment Staff

Assessment staffs are made up of management personnel two levels above that of the candidate being assessed and, thus, of supervisors of the level for which the assessees are candidates. In the case of vocation candidates for first-level management, second-level supervisors make up the assessment staff. Only occasionally have these staff members had any previous training in testing or assessment. Staffs undergo up to three weeks of training, the final week of which is a practice assessment of dry-run subjects.

The selection of candidates for assessment has nearly always been left to the regular appraisal processes operating in the organization. Management has been asked to send to the center only those they judge to possess the potential for immediate advancement into management. The high rejection rate of such candidates, has, therefore, come as a shock.

The assessment center has proven extremely attractive to line management as an adjunct to regular appraisal. Perhaps one reason for this attractiveness is that the process does not attempt to substitute for management judgment a mechanical probablity device such as forced-choice ratings, cutting scores on paper-and-pencil tests, or a predetermined pattern of abilities. Managerial judgment is the cornerstone of the process. The members of the assessment staff are from that level of management which has always had a strong voice in such promotions. In addition, the staff is given no mechanical methods for combining their many observations into any sort of final index. On the contrary, they are told that the weight accorded to any quality will depend on their own knowledge of the job and their experience as managers. The difference in making such judgments as a member of an assessment staff rather than out on the line is that the assessor sees all candidates, sees them all in standardized situations, and considers the same behavior as the other staff members. In addition, the 20 or so qualities which accessors are taught to consider open up a broader range of considerations that they may have previously had in mind.

Using the assessment center to select first-level managers from among current employees greatly enhances the quality of those admitted into the pool of future middle and upper managers. The majority of higher management comes, however, from the college graduates who are recruited specifically for their seeming potential for middle and upper management.

Assessment of College Recruits

We have not, so far, used the assessment center in college recruiting. There are a number of reasons for this. Perhaps chief among them is the fear that busy college seniors already spending much time in interviewing with many possible employers would not be willing to spend two days in being assessed. We have, nevertheless, found certain techniques short of full assessment valuable. Chief among these are the use of rank in college graduating class, mental ability test score, and a motivational interview on a pre-employment basis. Upon employment, the recruit enters our Initial Management Development Program (IMDP). The main purpose of this program is to confront the recruit with challenging assignments to speed his development, but another important feature is intensive appraisal of the young man's performance. If this appraisal does not support the assumption on which he was hired, that he is at least middle management material, he is asked to leave. The first year of work, therefore, backstops misses in pre-employment evaluation.

Although the above steps have greatly improved the calibre of our young college educated managers over what it was 10 years ago, we are not yet satisfied. One step we are about to take in the New York Telephone Company is to put our college recruits through a two-day assessment center shortly after they report for work. The results will be used to supplement the Initial Management Development Program appraisals to make more accurate judgments about who to keep beyond the initial year. Another approach, which is likely to be tried somewhere in the Bell System soon, is to select the most important techniques from the full assessment center to put together a half-day mini-assessment. This would be used on a pre-employment basis when the potential recruit visits the company.

The Importance of Using Assessment Centers

The use of assessment centers for the college and the non-college group can guarantee that a very high percentage of those in the management pool have good managerial abilities. This, to my mind, goes very far toward assuring total good management for an organization. Our research in the Management Progress Study has shown that the more capable men do in fact get identified by ordinary appraisal methods and moved into middle management first. The problem is that they then are followed into middle management by less capable men with inadequate abilities.

Companies that make a practice of hiring experienced men directly into middle management have an even greater need to apply assessment-center methods. The potential new employee is being brought in at a substantial level and salary, and there has been no chance, except rarely, to have observed him functioning in a managerial role. Especially careful pre-employment screening is necessary. That this is realized is attested to by the frequent practice of sending such candidates to consultants specializing in executive appraisal. These consultants usually limit their methods to the interview and paper-and-pencil tests. Although our research has demonstrated that such methods can be of genuine value in selection, we are also convinced that behavior simulations add a lot.

A major complicating factor in management selection, whether from within or without, is that of technical competence. Many positions that are managerial in level do not require management ability but, rather, special knowledge and skill. Examples readily come to mind from such fields as engineering, accounting, marketing, etc. Such specialized competence is frequently cited in urging the employment or advancement of candidates who, it is admitted, have low management potential. It is often asserted that these men are being taken on or promoted as specialists and that their lack of managerial ability is of no consequence. This sounds convincing but all too often such reservations are forgotten within a few years and the man is moved into even higher and truly managerial jobs just as readily as his peers.

The ideal way to avoid this is to hire or promote only those specialists who also have general managerial abilities. This ideal is almost impossible to carry out in practice. There just aren't enough triple-threat men. My suggestion is that steps be taken, such as putting prominent notes in personnel files, to insure that it not be forgotten that the individual reached his level of management only because of technical knowledge. This does not mean that he could not later be examined for general managerial ability by an assessment center.

I have not presented the research data we have accumulated about the assessment-center process. I have also ignored for the most part other methods of locating managers. This does not mean that I believe that assessment centers can be used as the sole method of management appraisal. I am, however, convinced that other methods are sufficiently weak so that they clearly need a strong supplement. I know of no other supplement as powerful as the assessment center.

Suggested Readings

1. Robert C. Albrook, "How To Spot Executives Early," *Fortune* (July, 1968), pp. 106-111.

2. D. W. Bray and D. L. Grant, "The Assessment Center in the Measurement of Potential for Business Management," *Psychological Monographs*, LXXX (1966).

3. D. W. Bray, "The Assessment Center Method of Appraising Management Potential," in *The Personnel Job in a Changing World*, ed. J.W. Blood (New York: American Management Association, 1964).

4. D. W. Bray, "The Management Progress Study," *American Psychologist*, XIX (1964), 419-420.

5. D. W. Bray and R. J. Campbell, "Selection of Salesmen by Means of an Assessment Center," *Journal of Applied Psychology*, LII (1968), 36-41.

6. R. J. Campbell and D. W. Bray, "Assessment Centers: An Aid in Management Selection," *Personnel Administration*, XXX (1967), 6-13.

7. D. L. Grant, W. Katkovsky, and D. W. Bray, "Contributions of Projective Techniques to Assessment of Management Potential," *Journal of Applied Psychology*, LI (1967), 226-232.

8. D. L. Grant and D. W. Bray, "Contributions of the Interview to Assessment of Management Potential," *Journal of Applied Psychology*, LIII (1969), 24-34.

9. *Predicting Managerial Success*, ed. John A. Meyers, Jr. (Ann Arbor, Michigan: Foundation For Research on Human Behavior, 1968).

appendix two

Research Methodology

Applied behavioral research in industry is designed to provide insights into humans and organizations. These insights permit analysis and correction of problems within industry. It is our hope that this book will stimulate further research, both applied and basic, in the social sciences.

In addition to the case-study companies, we conducted direct research in five other firms. In these companies we secured the cooperation of key people, such as ranking executives and personnel directors, and conducted in-depth interviews. The interviews encompassed the major topics covered in this book including the degree of organizational objectivity, the self-interest and company interest displayed by the management team, the corporate expectations, the degree of unofficial actions, the classifications of promotables, the practice of the various forms of nepotism and other considerations.

Statistical information obtained included (1) the present level of the manager, (2) age, (3) number of years with the company, (4) number of years on present job, (5) sex, (6) line, staff, or combination line-staff assignment, (7) functional area, such as production or engineering, (8) formal education, (9) whether the manager had received special accelerated training, (10) his observed Actual Balance, (11) his classification and (12) his potential levels of advancement within the organization based on known plans and formal appraisals.

The managers also completed the Self-Interest (self-company interest balance) Form, the Company Interest (objectivity) Form, and the Classification Form. Included with these forms was a letter of explanation and instruction. The letters and forms were distributed within the companies and after completion were mailed direct to the researchers in stamped, self-addressed envelopes provided by the researchers. No information was included on the forms which would permit identification of the manager.

In addition, we held in-depth interviews with members of the management teams in all eight companies, and in some cases, such as Diversified, we interviewed the complete management team. In a medium-sized chemical company, for example, we spent a great deal of time with the complete management team and arranged for completion of questionnaires by individuals, group evaluations of all individuals, and evaluations of all management people by the personnel director. In one of the largest companies in the United States we arranged for a detailed analysis of the management team and the organization.

We also conducted in-depth interviews of individuals in eight other major companies, the results of which supported the findings in the companies researched.

The results of this research provided the basis for a comprehensive questionnaire covering unofficial actions, the personal image, horizontal and vertical cliques, socionepotism and adoptive nepotism, the grapevine, executive isolation, the classifications of promotables, and corporate objectivity. This questionnaire was completed by a top executive in major firms selected from a sampling of *Fortune's* 500. Spaces were provided for comments on each topic, and many executives also wrote lengthy responses expressing their views.

We selected twelve major firms with a combined total of over 100,000 managers as the basis of our research findings for industry in general. These firms provided a representative sampling, and the results correlated with those of the other firms researched.

The contributing firms were quite receptive to the research conducted and in many cases top executives offered detailed information on their company's operations and philosophies with no restrictions on the use of this information. This was voluntarily generalized by the authors to preserve the anonymity of the firms and individual managers, since such identification could serve no useful purpose. The lower- and middle-level managers also often discussed their companies with complete candor.

The methods of appraisal used are not intended to be completely scientific in nature or in statistical accuracy. Instead they reflect tendencies or trends in behavior and practices and should be viewed as instructional behavioral tools. They are valid within the limitations of the perspectives of those participating and the methods employed. They provide insights that can increase individual and corporate objectivity and insights that can more closely equate individual and corporate goals.

index

A

Abdicator, 29
Actual balance (AB), 8–9
  classification and, 177
  promotability and, 178–181
  ratings
    at Amalgamated, 37, 177
    at Diversified, 40
    at Wildcat, 33
Adoptive nepotism, 63–64, 78, 136
Amalgamated Electronics, Inc.
  background of, 36–39
  dictators at, 36, 116–121, 177
  executives at, 37, 168–169, 177
  manager's actual balance and classification, 177
  manager's classification and promotability, 178
  organization chart of, 37
  promotability
    by actual balances, 181
    of classifications, 179
  subculture of, 47–49
  technicians at, 38, 105–107, 177
American Telephone and Telegraph assessment centers, 192–194, 197–205
Authority, actual vs. defined, 81–82
Avery, Sewell, 22

B

Basket case, 113
Bell Telephone system, 185
Big family effect, 45
Bray, Douglas W., 197
Bureaucracy, 74–77, 78
Busted-britches effect, 86

C

Classifications of managers, 17–30
  actual balance (AB) and, 177–178
  at Amalgamated Electronics Co., 37
  at Diversified Mfg. Co., 40
  promotability and, 178–180
  at Wildcat Petroleum Co., 33
Cliques, 78
  communication in, 60–61
  horizontal, 58–61
  municipal, 85
  opportunistic, 58–61
  promotability and, 58, 61
  vertical, 58–61
Communication
  in cliques, 60–61
  filtered, 71–72
  one-way, 76, 115
  skills, 84
  See also Grapevine